D1296717

Reflections of Honor
The Untold Story of a Nisei Spy

Lorraine Ward

Katherine Erwin

with

Yoshinobu Oshiro

Curriculum Research & Development Group
College of Education
University of Hawai'i at Mānoa

Curriculum Research & Development Group
University of Hawai'i at Mānoa
Honolulu

© 2014 Curriculum Research & Development Group
University of Hawai'i
All rights reserved
Printed in the United States of America

ISBN 978-1-58351-146-6

Curriculum Research & Development Group Staff
Kathleen F. Berg, Director
Thanh Truc T. Nguyen, Associate Director
Helen O. Au, Assistant Director
Morris K. Lai, Project Director
Lorraine Ward, Managing Editor
Katherine Erwin, Editorial Assistant
Susanne DeVore, Editorial Assistant
Amy Ngo, Editorial Assistant
Jaret K. C. Leong, Production Coordinator
Jana Shiraishi, Marketing Coordinator

Cover Design by Wayne M. Shishido
Layout and Design by Darrell T. Asato

Distributed by the
Curriculum Research & Development Group
College of Education
University of Hawai'i at Mānoa
1776 University Ave.
Honolulu, HI 96822

crdg@hawaii.edu
http://manoa.hawaii.edu/crdg/

This project

was undertaken in collaboration with and at the request of the Military Intelligence Service (MIS) Veterans of Kaua'i, with major preliminary work having been done by Quentin Belles, Yoshinobu Oshiro, Rosemary Komori Anzai, and Hideo Anzai. Oshiro was the bridge that connected the MIS Veterans of Kaua'i and this project to the Curriculum Research & Development Group (CRDG). An MIS veteran himself and a member of the MIS Veterans of Hawai'i, Oshiro was invited by Quentin Belles to become a member of the MIS Veterans of Kaua'i after the two met at a ceremony on the USS *Missouri.* Once part of the Kaua'i group, Oshiro learned about Arthur Komori and about the group's wish to create a permanent record of his story. Oshiro also had a longtime association with CRDG, both before and after his retirement from the Department of Education. In 2011, he approached Morris Lai and asked for assistance in writing and publishing a book about Arthur Komori. Several of us at CRDG immediately saw the historical importance of Komori's activities and were eager to help. This book is the result of that collaboration.

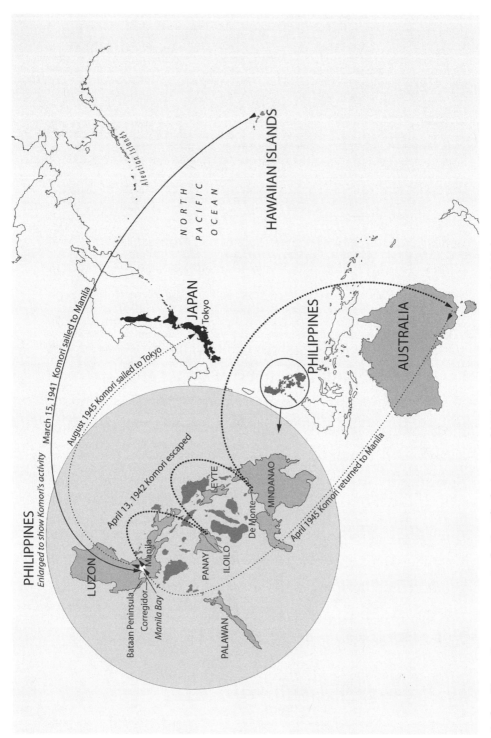

Arthur Komori's movements in the Pacific during World War II (Map by Wayne Shishido)

Contents

Timeline   vi

List of Acronyms   viii

List of Illustrations   ix

Foreword   xiii

Preface   xvii

CHAPTER 1   The Making of a Patriot   1

CHAPTER 2   Date with Destiny   7

CHAPTER 3   In War and Peace   53

CHAPTER 4   Enemies both Foreign and Domestic   91

CHAPTER 5   A Lifetime of Loyalty   105

Bibliography   117

Index   121

Timeline: Arthur Satoshi Komori

1915 **August 25,** Born

1935 Graduated from McKinley High School

1940 Graduated from University of Hawai'i

1941 **March 13,** Komori and Sakakida recruited into US Army, CIC

1941 **April 7,** Komori and Sakakida left for the Philippines

1941 **April,** Arrived in Manila

1941 **December 7,** Japan attacked Pearl Harbor, Territory of Hawai'i

1941 **December 8,** Japan attacked Manila, Philippines (December 7 in Hawai'i)

1941 **December 24,** G2 (Intelligence) evacuated from Manila to Bataan

1941 **December 26,** Manila declared an Open City

1942 **April 13,** Komori evacuated from Corregidor to Australia

1942 **May 7,** Reported missing in action

1942 **September,** ATIS formed, first class of MISLS graduates arrived in Australia

1943 **January,** Komori attended Field Security Section (FSS) School, Brisbane

1943 **September,** Attended CIC School, Brisbane

1943 **December to 1944 February,** Attended MISLS, Camp Savage, Minnesota

1944 **October 31,** Received permission to marry Marie N. Poon

1945 **April 6,** Komori returned to Manila

1945 **August 15,** Emperor broadcasts Imperial Rescript on the Termination of War

1945 **August 26,** Komori left Manila for Tokyo

1945 **August 31,** Arrived in Tokyo Bay for surrender

1945 **September 2,** Japan surrendered

1945 **September 3,** Komori entered Tokyo

1945 **November 3,** Returned to Hawai'i

1945 **December,** Awarded the Bronze Star for service in Manila

1945 **December 8,** Reenlisted as M/Sgt. in the 401st CIC Detachment, Honolulu, T.H.

1948 **January 9 to May 6,** Served as a security agent for atomic tests at Eniwetok Atoll

1949 **November to March 1952,** Taught at the CIC School, Camp Holabird, Baltimore, Maryland

1952 Resigned from the Army, became a Captain in the Air Force Reserve

1952 **to 1956,** Taught at CIC School as a civilian instructor

1952 **to 1954,** Attended law school at University of Maryland

1956 Returned to Hawai'i

1958 Passed Hawai'i bar exam

1959 **July to August,** Served as Hawai'i Deputy Attorney General

1988 **July 1,** Inducted into Military Intelligence Corps Hall of Fame

2000 **February 17,** Died

2000 **April 3,** MIS awarded the Presidential Unit Citation with two Oak Leaf Clusters by Louis Caldera, Secretary of the Army, for "extraordinary heroism in military operations against an armed enemy"

2011 **November 2,** Members of MIS, 442nd, and 100th Battalion awarded the Congressional Gold Medal by President Barack Obama

List of Acronyms

ATIS	Allied Translator and Interpreter Section
CIC	Counter Intelligence Corps
CIP	Corps of Intelligence Police
FSS	Field Security Section
G2	The Intelligence branch of the US Army
GHQ	General Headquarters
ILWU	International Longshore and Warehouse Union
MIS	Military Intelligence Service
MISLS	Military Intelligence Service Language School
NCO	Non-commissioned officer
ONI	Office of Naval Intelligence
POW	Prisoner of war
ROTC	Reserve Officer Training Corps
SCAP	Supreme Commander for the Allied Powers
SWPA	Southwest Pacific Area
TDY	Temporary duty yonder (a temporary duty assignment)
USAFIA	United States Army Forces in Australia
USASOS	United States Army Services of Supply

List of Illustrations

President William McKinley High School   1

USAT *Republic* in Honolulu Harbor   7

Radiogram authorizing Komori's original enlistment   10

Komori's swearing in at Fort Shafter, Honolulu   12

USAT *Republic* ready to sail   14

Manila in November 1941   16

The Japanese district in Manila in November 1941   17

Fort Santiago   19

Komori's journal entry for the morning of December 8, 1941   22

Old Bilibid Prison   24

Komori in uniform   26

Map of Manila Bay with Komori's movements in 1941–1942   30

Japanese bombers over Corregidor   31

Anti-aircraft artillery on Corregidor   31

Manila declared an "open city"   32

General Jonathan M. Wainwright   35

Members of the Japanese Kempeitai   35

Frank Hachiya   37

General Douglas MacArthur with Major General Richard K. Sutherland   39

Interior of Malinta Tunnel   42

Soldiers emerging from Malinta Tunnel   45

Komori's journal entry describing his escape from Corregidor   49

Paul I. "Pappy" Gunn   50

B-25 bombers in flight   52

53   B-25 bombers on the deck of the USS *Hornet*

59   Major General Charles A. Willoughby

64   ATIS translators

65   Australian Aborigine

67   MISLS students at Camp Savage, Minnesota

70   Article published in the *Honolulu Star-Bulletin*

73   MacArthur wading ashore at Leyte, Philippines

73   Sunken Japanese ships in Manila Bay

76   Richard Sakakida

78   Internment camp at Manzanar

83   Surrender ceremony aboard the USS *Missouri*

84   Instrument of Surrender

85   Instrument of Surrender

86   General MacArthur exiting the Daiichi Building, Tokyo

87   Samurai sword presented to Komori by MacArthur

91   Japanese district of Honolulu in 1950

93   Secretary General Tokuda of the Japanese Communist Party

98   Jiro Yukimura

101   Nuclear testing at Eniwetok Atoll

102   CIC School at Fort Holabird, Maryland

105   Presidential Unit Citation ceremony, April 2000

107   Japanese Americans waiting to board a train to an internment camp

109   Commendation from Brigadier General Thorpe

113   President Bill Clinton awarding the Presidential Unit Citation

114   Congressional Gold Medal

114   President Barrack Obama signing the bill authorizing the Congressional Gold Medal

Umi no oya yori, sodate no oya.

The parents who raised you take precedence over the parents to whom you were born.

This Japanese proverb captures well Komori's outlook with regard to his loyalty to America from very early in his life. It also describes the dilemma of Japanese Americans of Issei parents with regards to their loyalty, either to the country of their birth (USA) or the country of their parents' birth (Japan).

生みの親より育ての親

.

Foreword

The first Japanese immigrants to Hawai'i arrived in 1868 as contract laborers for the sugar plantations. By 1910, approximately 10,000 Nisei (second-generation Japanese) had been born in Hawai'i. By 1920, Hawai'i-born Nisei numbered about 50,000, nearly half of the 110,000 Japanese in Hawai'i. By the 1940s there were 160,000 Japanese in Hawai'i, of whom 120,000 were Nisei. One of these was Arthur Komori, born on Maui in 1915. He attended public elementary and high schools and the University of Hawai'i. He participated in youth activities, sports, and Boy Scouts, as well as other social and religious organizations.

When World War II began in 1941, suddenly not just the loyalty, but even the nationality of these American Nisei was in question. The Nisei's nationality—that is, their citizenship—was determined by the laws of both Japan and the United States. In the United States, nationality was, and still is, determined by birthplace—the Nisei born in the United States were American citizens by birthright. But under Japanese law, nationality had traditionally been based on bloodline; that is, any child of a Japanese father, regardless of birthplace, was a Japanese citizen. With the large number of Nisei born to Japanese parents in Hawai'i and on the US mainland in the early twentieth century, the issue had become one of intense diplomatic discussion between the two nations, and Japan had begun to address the issue with an amendment to its laws in 1924 that allowed for the expatriation of foreign-born Japanese citizens. In the 1930s, as storm clouds brewed over Asia and the Pacific, Japanese Foreign Minister Yosuke Matsuoka had visited Hawai'i, and he urged the Nisei of Hawai'i to be loyal to the country of their birth, quoting the Japanese proverb "Umi no oya yori, sodate no oya" (The parents who raised you take precedence over the parents to whom you were born). Nevertheless, the fact remained that at the moment that war began between Japan and the United States, Japan considered the 120,000 Hawai'i-born Nisei citizens of Japan while the United States considered them American citizens, and this legal issue of their dual citizenship would haunt the Nisei throughout the war.

While Arthur Komori's upbringing, and his later writings, indicated no ambiguity about his allegiance and loyalty to the United States, he was nevertheless one of those who found himself, through no fault of his own, under suspicion. And like so many others of his generation, by the end of the war, he had proven his loyalty, honor, and patriotism for the country of his birth beyond any doubt. But Komori's story has another twist to it, one that distinguishes him from his fellow Nisei. He was one of the first Nisei recruited into the US Army, even before the war started, for deployment in the Counter Intelligence Corps (CIC). Komori worked for the CIC undercover in pre-war Manila to gather information that would help the United States prepare for war. When war came, he worked as a translator and undercover agent on the front lines in Bataan, in danger of being branded a traitor by Japan if he had been captured, and in danger of misidentification by American soldiers since Japanese Americans were, at that time, still forbidden from enlisting in the US Army. Kauaʻi Military Intelligence Service (MIS) Veteran's Service Club president Quentin Belles called Komori "a unique individual whose secret and one-of-a-kind contributions to his beloved country in time of brutal combat were always made in silence, and often, in deadly peril."

It was in part because of the political climate and in part because of the secret nature of his work that the story of Arthur Komori's military career has never been told, and the telling of this hero's story that has few, if any, parallels is long overdue. In 1943, General MacArthur's Chief of Intelligence, General Charles A. Willoughby, wrote of Komori, "Sgt. Komori's service in peace and war has been of the highest order and I can recommend him to your favorable attention." With this book, we are thrilled, at long last, to make his story available to the public, so that finally, we also can "recommend him to your favorable attention."

Yoshinobu Oshiro
Honolulu, Hawaiʻi
October 2013

Preface

In working on this book, I have often felt that the person who should have written this story was Arthur Komori himself. This biography tells the story of a true patriot who spent his life in service to his country, even in the face of suspicion and prejudice. It also shows us a man who recorded his thoughts about the events he was a part of in poetry and prose. We have copies of much of his writing—all of it unpublished, so we have tried to use his own words to tell his story whenever we could. Throughout the book you will see many passages in quotation marks with no reference to a source. They are typically introduced by phrases like "in his own words" and "as Komori later wrote." These passages are quoted from Komori's own writing—everything from handwritten journals from his days in Bataan and Corregidor to official reports and memos to memoirs he wrote as late as 1989 to an oral history interview he gave in 1992. Arthur Komori was also a poet, and we have included his poetry throughout the book to provide his firsthand impression of events as they were going on.

Komori's papers include two sets of materials. The first is his own accounts of events, often written on site as the events he described were happening. He also wrote many informal memoirs over the years, both summarizing the details of his military career and reflecting on the events he had lived through.

The other category can be summarized as official documents. These include copies of orders from the army authorizing recruitment or assignments, recommendations for decoration (most often denied), and other official army correspondence.

The records of the MIS were sealed for three decades after the war, and were not made publicly available until the passage of the Freedom of Information Act of 1974. Much of the story still is available only through persistent digging, and there is much that has not yet come to light. Because of this long delay, stories about the MIS and their role in the war—each of which adds substantially to the bigger picture—are still being written. More and more of this story is coming out every year. Because of this, we consider this biography a work in progress. We are excited to be able to tell Arthur Komori's story. But we understand that at some time in the future, an expanded and more complete version of this story may be possible, and we urge all interested readers to keep digging and learning about these brave men and to keep working to make their stories known.

Lorraine Ward
Honolulu, Hawai'i
October 2013

CHAPTER 1

The Making of a Patriot

President William McKinley High School (Courtesy of Joel Bradshaw)

When the story of the contribution made by the Nisei, or second-generation Japanese Americans, to the United States' World War II victory in the Pacific is told, it usually begins with the bombing of Pearl Harbor. It unfolds with the backlash of suspicion this event triggered and the subsequent internment of Japanese Americans, before moving on to the US government's change of heart, when it allowed the formation of the predominately Nisei 100th Battalion and 442nd Regimental Combat Team in 1942 and 1944 respectively. Today, the great valor, sacrifice, and patriotism of the men who served in those units in the European theater of war are well known.

But there is another chapter to the story of the Nisei's service in World War II—one that begins much earlier than December 7, 1941 and that, even today, is not widely known. The Nisei who served the United States in the Pacific were involved in the war from the beginning, and in a few cases, before the beginning, and they worked long and hard, often in isolation, and always in great danger because of their ancestry, to prove to all Americans that they were loyal Americans, too. Arthur Komori's part in this story began when he was twenty-five years old and a graduate of the University of Hawai'i. Komori was fresh out of college and employed as a clerk at the Bonded Realty Company in Honolulu when, unbeknownst to him, events were happening behind the scenes that would change his life irrevocably. He later wrote of that turning point in his life that it was "a heaven-sent opportunity to prove ourselves." Komori would go on to serve his country with outstanding valor throughout the war and into the postwar period, a pioneer in a group of Nisei that would come to be known for their patriotism and bravery.

The Early Years

Arthur Satoshi Komori was born to Esther Kyoko Komori and Yoshitaro Komori on August 25, 1915 in Haʻikū, Maui. He was the second oldest of seven children, with sisters Aiko, Mary, Martha, Portia, and Viola, and brother David. The family moved around the Territory of Hawaiʻi to accommodate their father's role as a foreman at the American Can Company, residing at seven different addresses during Arthur's childhood. By his middle school years, the family had settled on Oʻahu, where he attended Central Intermediate School and McKinley High School.

Komori's young life was full of a wide range of activities that provided him with the opportunity to develop the skills he would later draw on in his military work. One of the most important of these was the Japanese language classes he attended in the afternoons after his public school classes from the age of six to seventeen. This practice was common for second-generation Japanese American, or Nisei, children as a means of retaining the language and culture of their parents' homeland in a foreign environment (Komori's father had been born in Japan, and his mother, of Japanese descent, had been born in Hawaiʻi). Indeed, this practice of attending Japanese language school outside of their regular schooling continues for many Japanese American children today.

Besides taking language classes, Komori also belonged to the Boy Scouts, the Nuʻuanu YMCA, the American Legion, the Hawaii Pigeon Association, and the Church of the Crossroads. In high school, he was a member of the McKinley Science Club, the McKinley Chemical Fraternity, the McKinley Honor Society, and McKinley's Reserve Officer Training Corps (ROTC). Komori was also involved in the Honolulu Junior Chamber of Commerce and was an avid chess player. He even found time for a job as a stacker at the American Can Company.

Following his graduation from McKinley High School in 1935, Komori attended the University of Hawaiʻi (UH), where his studies focused on English, Japanese, and social science, culminating in a pre-law degree in 1940. Throughout his academic career, Komori showed a wide range of interests and was active both at school and in the community. His interest in science continued at the university where he was a member of the American Astronomical Society. Komori also continued as an ROTC cadet at UH and, for four months in 1940, attended the Civil Aviation Academy (CAA) Flight School at UH as well as K-T Flight School, where he earned a private pilot's license. He was also a four-year letterman, captain of the university swim team, and a state champion in backstroke. And, as he had in high school, he found time in his busy schedule to hold down a part-time job, this time as a service station attendant. Later in life, Komori cited his UH swim captaincy, Boy Scout training under C. Dudley Pratt, pilot training at the University of Hawai'i, and college degree as his only background and qualifications upon entering the army.

It is easy to think of the war as the precipitating event that forced all Nisei to choose between loyalty to the US, their homeland, and some, even vestigial, interest in or loyalty to the land of their ancestors. In Komori's case, at least, that was not true. Although he had been raised in a Japanese household, his strong feelings about his identity as an American were already substantially formed by the time he left McKinley High School. Writing later in his life about the "Japanese-Americans of Hawai'i and the States," he noted that "we have, most all of us, sought in some manner or other to prove that we were Americans and also that we were loyal." He described his own efforts in that regard, which were not only pro-American, but also actively anti-Japanese:

> In my adolescent manner of thinking, I had decided at that early date [1935, the year he graduated from McKinley High School] to become truly American . . . . I never joined any racial clubs at the University of Hawaii. I had alienated myself from Japanese institutions to such an extent, that when I was plunged into the Japanese community of Manila in 1941 in my secret mission, I had to make a supreme effort to adopt things Japanese again.

He also described his simultaneous efforts to prove himself an American: "The first step I took in young manhood to prove my Americanism was to legalize my Christian name in 1935." In 1936, he tried to join the Hawai'i National Guard as part of a recruiting drive but was refused. He tried again after earning his private pilot's certificate, applying in 1940 for the Army Air Force Cadet Flight Training, but was, in his words, "rejected by Washington after taking a physical and appearing before a board at Hickam Field." He wrote that, "the chips were stacked against me, but no one could say I had not tried." But he added that, "fate is not always unkind. The forces of an unseen hand had begun working in my favor."

CHAPTER 2

Date with Destiny

USAT Republic *at Pier 9, Honolulu Harbor* (Courtesy of the Naval History and Heritage Command)

In February 1941, ten months prior to the United States' involvement in WWII, recent UH graduate Arthur Komori was working hard as a clerk for the Bonded Realty Company during the day and as a bartender at the Kapaakea Grill at night. Neither of these jobs was Komori's first choice of employment. With his background in ROTC, Komori was determined to join the military, despite the rejections he had already received. He was fit, intelligent, and dedicated—there was no reason, other than his ethnicity, for him to be refused.

Anti-Japanese sentiment in the United States did not begin with the bombing of Pearl Harbor. It had been growing in the West for most of the twentieth century. In 1941, Japan had been on an empire-building mission for about a decade, and its territorial holdings encompassed the Sakhalin Peninsula and Kurile Island to the north; Bonin Island to the southeast; the Ryukyu Islands and Taiwan to the southwest; and the Korean Peninsula, Manchuria (where they had set up a friendly puppet government), Shanghai, Beijing, and Nanjing to the west. Japan's Kwantung Army officially entered into war with Chiang Kai-shek's Chinese forces in 1937, although they had been fighting since 1931.

Empire building needs resources, and many of Japan's resources came from the United States. However, the United States had placed an embargo on steel and iron exports on September 22, 1940, when Japan launched its invasion of French Indochina. To add further pressure, Great Britain had opened the previously closed Burma Road, providing an important supply line for the Chinese. Japan then signed the Tripartite Pact with Germany and Italy on September 27, 1940, formalizing their alliance and pledging mutual assistance should any of the signatories be attacked by any nation not already involved in the war.

As tension continued to escalate, the United States realized that it needed American spies who could blend into the tight-knit Japanese community. Despite the prevailing anti-Japanese sentiment that kept Japanese Americans like Komori out of the armed forces, on February 19, 1941, a radiogram was received in Fort Shafter, Honolulu from the War Department in Washington, DC, that granted authority for the "original enlistment of two American citizens of Japanese extraction."

A search for the right people commenced immediately. Komori and Richard Sakakida, a fellow Nisei and McKinley graduate several years Komori's junior, together with thirty other candidates, were invited to test for these two spots. The enlistment officer for Komori and Sakakida was Major Jack Gilbert, who had trained both men as the ROTC instructor at McKinley. There are few details in Komori's journals and memoirs about the interview process, but Sakakida described it in detail in his biography, *A Spy in Their Midst*. The process began with the initial call from Major Gilbert, asking him to report to Central Intermediate School the next morning. As Sakakida remembered it, "although I had no remaining ties with ROTC, I felt I was receiving an order that I could not refuse."

Upon his arrival, Sakakida told his biographer, he was "surprised to see uniformed army and navy officers who, with nary an introduction or explanation, started questioning

Peggy

CONFIDENTIAL

RADIO FROM TAG

65 WD KI WAR 65

WASHINGTON DC   FEB 19 1941 1030

COMMANDING GENERAL HAW DEPT
FT SHAFTER TH

639 NINETEENTH   IN REPLY CITE TWO ONE EIGHT NAUGHT ELEVENTH FEB NINETEEN

AG&A
FORTY ONE, AUTHORITY GRANTED FOR ORIGINAL ENLISTMENT OF TWO AMERICAN CITI

for transfer
ZENS OF JAPANESE EXTRACTION TO PHILLIPINE DEPT IN GRADE OF SERGEANT COMMA

SAILING ON NEXT TRANSPORT TWENTY SECOND MARCH

ADAMS

A PARAPHRASED COPY

M W Marston
M.W. MARSTON
Lt. Colonel, G.S.C.
A.C. of S., G-2

CONFIDENTIAL

This radiogram authorizing the enlistment of two Japanese Americans arrived at Fort Shafter in Honolulu in February 1941.

me." The interview panel consisted of six officers, and the interview, which lasted the whole day, was followed by three full days of language testing. Sakakida described the interview as "a grueling process that left me exhausted at the end of each day." After the four days of tests, both young men returned to their jobs, still with no idea what they had been interviewed for.

Two weeks later, Komori and Sakakida each got a call from Major Gilbert offering his congratulations. They had been chosen from the thirty-plus candidates to enter the Corps of Intelligence Police (CIP, later known as Counter Intelligence Corps, or CIC). At this point, neither man knew what that service would entail. "We had volunteered," wrote Komori, "without the faintest knowledge of our mission, destination, or Army status. The lures of adventure, travel, and good clothes were incentives enough." While this comment undoubtedly reflects the excitement of a young man about to embark on an adventure, he also wrote, "that we had been chosen for our loyalty, we had no doubts, and we felt honored. Above all, we wanted to prove worthy of the high trust placed in us," a much more serious sentiment that was reflected in his actions and writings throughout his army career. Komori also recognized the impact that his enlistment and subsequent performance would have on his fellow Japanese Americans: "As the first Japanese-Americans to be chosen for such a secret mission, we felt keenly our

Arthur Komori is sworn in as a member of the Corps of Intelligence Police of the US Army on March 13, 1941 at Fort Shafter in Honolulu.

responsibility for the sake of our fellow Japanese-Americans, for the sake of Hawaii, and for the sake of our alien parents."

Following their swearing in at Fort Shafter on March 13, 1941, the two new recruits were promoted from Private to Sergeant and told to be ready for a secret mission. They could reveal to their immediate family that they were going to Manila but could give no further details. They were even misled initially as to the nature of their assignment, having been informed that the CIP was the Civilian Interpreter Police. It was actually the Corps of Intelligence Police, a part of the US Army's G2 (Intelligence) Division, responsible not simply for translating documents, but for acquiring information, often from behind enemy lines. In a personal memoir written in 1989, Komori described his lack of qualifications for the job he was about to undertake but concluded, "the FBI check must have cleared us, for we were on our way." So, with a history that included high school ROTC, a swim captaincy, Japanese language skills, a pre-law degree, and a private pilot's license, Komori eagerly embarked on a new life that would prove to be full of both unforeseeable dangers and incredible successes.

The two new CIP agents, still without any details on what their assignment would be, went undercover from the moment they left Honolulu, signing on as civilian crew members aboard the USAT *Republic*, which was carrying an Army National Guard unit from New Mexico bound for Manila. Only the ship's captain knew Komori's and Sakakida's identities, and the two men were ordered not to fraternize with anyone except the crew. Their recruitment, enlistment, and transport had been so swift and so secret that speculation about the odd circumstances of their departure began to spread throughout Honolulu. In a 1999 interview, a group of Komori's fellow MIS veterans described the "vilification and deprecating rumors" about Komori that circulated around Honolulu. They noted, in particular, the

Arthur Komori and Richard Sakakida left Honolulu aboard the USAT Republic, *pictured here. Already in their undercover roles, the two newly minted agents signed on as civilian crew.* (Courtesy of the Naval History and Heritage Command)

rumor that Komori had joined the Japanese army as a pilot and had been shot down at Pearl Harbor wearing a Japanese uniform and his McKinley High School class ring.

As the *Republic* approached Manila, Komori and Sakakida were met by Captain Nelson Raymond, commanding officer of the CIP in the Philippines, who approached the USAT *Republic* in a private launch three miles off the Manila coastline. At this first meeting with Captain Raymond, who would become one of Komori's earliest and most valued mentors, the two new sergeants were each handed an envelope and told to read the instructions therein and then to destroy the contents. In this way, they learned that they would not be monitoring Japanese radio broadcasts and newspapers, as they had initially believed. They discovered instead that the CIP, the counter-intelligence arm of the US Army, whose mission was "the detection of treason, sedition, subversive activity, and disaffection and the detection, prevention, or neutralization of espionage and sabotage," had selected them with a far more dangerous mission in mind—to go undercover in the Japanese business community of Manila.

The Manila where Komori and Sakakida arrived in April 1941 was a bustling metropolis. The Philippines had been a US colony since 1898 when the United States seized the archipelago from Spain following approximately five hundred years of Spanish rule. In 1935, it was made a commonwealth, and a ten-year plan for its independence was established. Because of its location, it became a strategic stronghold in 1941. The Japanese had a much longer history in the Philippines, having traded there since pre-colonial times, and during the era of Spanish rule, a wave of Christian Japanese immigrants fleeing religious persecution in Japan had settled in the Manila area. In the twentieth century, many Japanese immigrated to work on the plantations. It is estimated

This shot of bustling downtown Manila was featured in a Life *magazine photo-essay of Manila in November 1941.* (Courtesy of Getty Images)

that there were between 100,000 and 200,000 Japanese in the Philippines at the time of World War II. Komori and Sakakida would spend the next seven months infiltrating the inner circles of the Japanese business community in Manila, securing the confidence of its businessmen and couriering valuable intelligence back to General Douglas MacArthur and his staff.

At their first discreet meeting with Captain Raymond once they had disembarked in Manila, Raymond gave Komori

and Sakakida each some cash, in pesos, and told them to find
lodgings—Komori at the Toyo Hotel and Sakakida at the
Nishikawa Hotel. "Only then did the magnitude of our task
dawn on us," wrote Komori. Captain Raymond "suggested
that we 'cook up' a story that we had jumped ship, and very
conveniently, the passenger liner SS *President Cleveland* was

This photo from Life *magazine shows Manila's Japanese district in November,
1941, when, according to Komori, Japanese businessmen were quietly sending
their wives and children back to Japan.* (Courtesy of Getty Images)

also in port." Komori added to that story "that I was a draft dodger, which was favorably received by the pro-Emperor sons of Japan." Apparently, word had not reached Manila that Japanese Americans were unlikely to have been drafted.

Neither of the two undercover Nisei was issued a military ID, and they were ordered to destroy any instructions given to them. They understood that the army would not take responsibility for them or admit their roles to anyone outside the intelligence division should they run into trouble. Komori and Sakakida were well aware that they took their lives into their own hands when they took on this mission. Komori's steadfast patriotism explained his easy acceptance of the situation: "I would die rather than reveal my role," he wrote, "to give my all for my country, for my parents, for the Hawaiian people was my objective."

Settled in at the Toyo Hotel with his cover story in place, Komori began searching for a job. Posing as a Japanese sympathizer, he worked at the Japan Tourist Bureau, the Domei News Agency (Japan's official World War II news service), and the Japanese Consulate. (He became so trusted there that, had the war not intervened, Komori would likely have become a regular staff member at the Japanese Consulate.) With this façade in place, he spent the summer and fall of 1941 engaged in the deadly serious game of surveillance, collecting and passing on information on the mindset and actions of the Japanese business community.

Fort Santiago, on the bayfront in Manila, housed the headquarters of the US Army's G2 (Intelligence) Unit in the months leading up to World War II. (Courtesy of the National Archives)

During this time, he and Sakakida kept in touch with the army mainly through a post office box at the Central Post Office that was registered under the Filipino name Sixto Borja (Borja was a common Filipino surname, and Sixto indicated Sakakida's code: B-16). Through the post office box, they received orders for rendezvous points and information on where to drop off reports for General MacArthur. Once a month, Komori was smuggled out of Manila by Captain Raymond or Grenfell Drisko, another CIC agent, the only people at the time who knew who Komori and Sakakida were and what their mission was. Once he was safely smuggled into the confines of the G2 office in Fort Santiago, Komori could collect his pay and deliver reports in person. Outside of these meetings, he was entirely on his own. Although Komori and Sakakida were in the same role, they worked entirely independently of each other. As Komori described it,

> Richard and I had the freedom of the town and were in every sense of the phrase 'on our own.' I was no stranger to the bright lights of Manila, but was careful not to be seen being too extravagant. We had to be ever on our guard and steadfast to our mission.

The stress involved in always maintaining their cover never let up, even when they were around their fellow Americans. Although American by birth, Komori could by no means count on being in the good graces of his countrymen given the poor impression established by his draft-dodger cover as well as the stigma surrounding his ethnicity. "Americans were no friends of ours," he wrote, and "the Filipinos were a questionable lot with many among them who thought nothing of selling information to the Japs."

Throughout this period, Captain Raymond was not just a contact but also an invaluable mentor. Teaching the two Nisei the subtle techniques of interrogation "in the best traditions of the CIP," Raymond passed on to the young men tools that helped keep them alive. Komori later wrote,

We had no previous training as agents. Captain Raymond intended that we appear as civilian as ever, without a trace of the G.I. in us. He even cautioned us against purchasing raincoats of olive-drab hue. He knew what he was about, for he had been an agent since World War I.

His training under Captain Raymond allowed Komori to successfully infiltrate the Japanese community in Manila and to provide invaluable intelligence in the months leading up to the war. But, as it turned out, Raymond's efforts to teach Komori how to extract information from the enemy were, at first, hardly necessary. Once Komori was accepted into society, the Japanese businessmen were quick to share their sentiments with him. Komori found them to be "even more subversively inclined than in Hawaii. So naturally there was much to investigate." Referring to them as "arrogant, expansionist minded, and secretive," he added that "their China successes had 'gone to their heads' and they felt assured of their future role in the Orient."

Collecting pivotal information from his vantage point as an insider, Komori learned such details as "when Japanese nationals began quietly shipping their families home...[and] when people began collecting survival kits." He reported that the Japanese were becoming increasingly impatient with the "weak-kneed" policies of the Konoye cabinet, and he was personally involved in "secret" planning by the Japanese to

marines at war.
Dec. 8, Woke up to the blaring tune of newsboys trumpeting, "Jaliba!" "Eptra!" Poked my head out the Toyo Hotel room window and had the boy throw up a paper. "Hawaii Bombed!" I could not believe that my fair, impregnable Hawaii had been bombed. I never believed this until, Philippine Constabulary soldiers, with fixed bayonets corralled me and a dozen others in the Domei Office, Crystal Arcade Bldg., Escolta St, Manila, and interned us at Bilibid Prison. An American among Japs. It was not so ridiculous, because I was to all outward appearances and actions a Jap, too. It was yet not time to reveal my true identity, so I stuck it out, even to the extent of being spitted on an enraged, rabid Filipino bayonet. The Japs were a bewildered, stunned crowd, who resignedly turned their eyes toward their Land of the Rising Sun. It was blood-red now — bloody!

Komori's journal entry for the morning of December 8, 1941, in Manila recorded his shock at the attack on his homeland.

evacuate to points of safety and ration out supplies in the
event of war. In November 1941, less than a month before the
bombing of Pearl Harbor and Manila, Komori warned that the
Japanese had evacuated all women and children to Japan and
that "we were told in the community too, that we should build
up our emergency supplies, flashlights, canned goods, matches,
clothing, and tenting materials. They were sure making ready
for something."

Even with all this evidence telling him that something
was coming, Komori still made this entry in his journal on
December 8:

> Woke up to the blaring tune of newsboys trumpeting
> "Talibo!" "Extra!" Poked my head out of the Toyo
> Hotel room window and had the boy throw up a
> paper. "Hawaii Bombed!" I could not believe that my
> fair, impregnable Hawaii had been bombed. I never
> believed this until Philippine Constabulary soldiers,
> with fixed bayonets corralled me and a dozen others
> in the Domei Office, Crystal Arcade Bldg., Escolta
> St., Manila, and interned us at Bilibid Prison.

Komori had become so well integrated into the
Japanese community in Manila that when war did break out,
with the bombing of Pearl Harbor on December 7, 1941, and
the subsequent bombing of Manila on December 8 (December 7
in Hawai'i), he was at the Domei News Agency offices drinking
sake toasts to Emperor Hirohito. By his own description,

Arthur Komori was imprisoned briefly in Old Bilibid Prison. He later called it "the hellhole of Manila" in his journal. (Courtesy of the Library of Congress)

this first encounter with war found him in the "most unenviable position of one who was Japanese by all outward appearance," surrounded by Filipino Constabularymen with fixed bayonets who took him to Bilibid Prison with the other Japanese nationals. Of his supposed fellow Japanese nationals Komori wrote, "they were a bewildered, stunned crowd, who resignedly turned their eyes toward their Land of the Rising Sun." He added that "it was yet not time to reveal my true identity, so I stuck it out, even to the extent of being spitted on an enraged rabid Filipino bayonet."

Despite the understanding that the army would not break his cover even to save his life, Komori was sure he would somehow make it out of Bilibid Prison, which he called "the hell-hole of Manila." He later wrote, "I had profound faith in the teachings of Captain Raymond, and no doubt about being secretly reinstated into his Corps—that is, if nothing happened to my skin by then." Confined to prison, Komori resolved to find out if the Japanese residents of Manila had been aware of plans for an attack on Pearl Harbor, or if they "were implicated in any dark designs for the conquest of the Philippines." In the following week, he discovered what he called the "arrogant and warlike mentality of the supposedly peaceful businessmen from Japan." However, he was able to determine that none of his fellow detainees had known about the attacks on either Pearl Harbor or Manila beforehand. He also learned that they were convinced of the invincibility of their forces, sure that they would soon be freed. Komori had been imprisoned for four days when he was rescued from Bilibid Prison by Agent Drisko on Captain Raymond's orders, and he wrote "once again I was able to lift my head proudly as a real-life American."

Following his rescue, Komori returned to the G2 unit at Fort Santiago, no longer undercover. But in those early stages of the war, even a US Army uniform didn't insulate him from suspicion or danger. Komori would later write in his memoirs that,

Once the war started, Komori's undercover role ceased, and he joined his fellow soldiers in uniform.

early in my CIP and CIC careers, I felt as one among thousands of whites, being of Japanese ancestry. So the feeling of being 'on the spot' wore off only gradually. I was not so naïve as to believe that people who hated the Japs so bitterly would readily accept me as being one of a totally different breed.

Sakakida had also, under orders from Captain Raymond, been detained with a group of Japanese nationals at the Nippon Club, a Japanese businessmen's club in Manila. Although the Filipino constabularymen checking him in found his passport and knew, therefore, that he was American, Sakakida asked to be allowed to stay, using the (legitimate) excuse that because he looked Japanese, he would be in danger of being shot if he were seen at large in Manila. Because of his voluntary status at the Nippon Club, he, unlike the Japanese nationals, was allowed to come and go, and on the third day of captivity, he was asked to go out to purchase milk and other perishable food for the children. In the course of this errand, he was arrested by the Filipino constabulary as a suspected Japanese spy. He, too, was eventually rescued from this captivity by Captain Raymond and found himself back at G2 headquarters and in uniform.

Now that the war had begun, Komori and Sakakida were plunged into a new role that involved any tasks that required Japanese language skills. Almost immediately, they were put to work interrogating Japanese prisoners of war. They conducted their first interrogation, of two Japanese naval aviators who had flown out of Formosa (now Taiwan), on December 15. Komori later wrote about the experience, explaining that although he initially felt what he described as a "weird sensation" when he came face-to-face with "human beings who were our enemies and a menace to civilization," he was also aware that they would be a valuable source of intelligence and were worth the effort of a thoughtful interrogation. Rather than holding on to a "feeling of intense hatred, we viewed them as some kind of wild animal. . . . We of the intelligence breed were more concerned with their thoughts and emotions, and their identities and reaction, from then on." On a more personal level, he said, "being human beings, what else could we do but treat them mercifully? Then and there we began our practice of treating

POWs kindly. . . . This practice produced intelligence news and dividends."

This practice produced such results because it was, in fact, a compelling form of psychological warfare. Japanese soldiers believed that it was a disgrace to be captured by the enemy, and Komori and Sakakida, who were running the interrogations together, were able to use this to their advantage. Because Japanese soldiers were trained to fight to the death, they had had no preparation or training for how they should act as prisoners or what they should do when interrogated. Although these POWs were ignorant of their rights under the Third Geneva Convention, their Nisei interrogators were not. Komori and Sakakida primed the prisoners by treating them with unexpected mercy, providing water, food, medical care, and cigarettes, then used the Japanese sense of honor against them. A common technique was to appear to accept the POWs' stories at face value during the initial interrogation, then find evidence from captured documents, military identification, or other prisoners' accounts that contradicted the prisoners' stories. Once confronted with these facts during subsequent interviews, the captured Japanese soldiers would usually break down in shame and tell the truth.

Komori later wrote the definitive report on the treatment and interrogation of Japanese POWs based on this method of using kindness and fact checking that he and Sakakida had developed in those first weeks of the war. The manual was used throughout the Pacific War and gave the Allies a great advantage in the intelligence arena, an advantage that was achieved through a unique combination of human decency, adherence to the Geneva Convention, and an insider's perspective on Japanese traditions of honor and duty.

While Komori and Sakakida were having success with their particular tasks, the war for Manila and the Philippines was not going well for the United States and its allies. In late December, President Franklin Delano Roosevelt ordered General MacArthur to leave the Philippines and proceed to Australia. Unbeknownst to General MacArthur, the decision had been made in Washington to follow a "Europe first" strategy, establishing the battle against Germany as the top priority and leaving troops in the Philippines without the support they required for success against overwhelming Japanese forces. The troops on the ground remained ignorant of this plan, and even General MacArthur disregarded the order to evacuate for months.

However, with Japan overtaking Manila by land, sea, and air, on December 23, 1941, General MacArthur did order a fallback of US forces to the Bataan Peninsula and Corregidor, an island in the mouth of Manila Bay. Late on December 24, the entire G2 office and its personnel, of which Komori and Sakakida, as CIP agents, were a part, were evacuated from Manila to Corregidor, also known as "the Rock." In his diary,

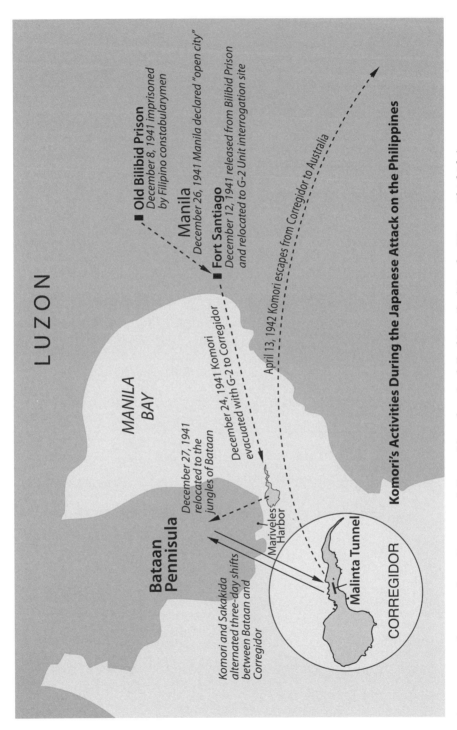

LUZON

MANILA BAY

Bataan Pennisula

■ Old Bilibid Prison
*December 8, 1941 imprisoned
by Filipino constabularymen*

Manila
December 26, 1941 Manila declared "open city"

■ Fort Santiago
*December 12, 1941 released from Bilibid Prison
and relocated to G-2 Unit interrogation site*

*December 27, 1941
relocated to the
jungles of Bataan*

*December 24, 1941 Komori
evacuated with G-2 to Corregidor*

April 13, 1942 Komori escapes from Corregidor to Australia

*Komori and Sakakida
alternated three-day shifts
between Bataan and
Corregidor*

Mariveles
Harbor

Malinta Tunnel

CORREGIDOR

Komori's Activities During the Japanese Attack on the Philippines

Komori spent four months on Bataan and Corregidor after the fall of Manila. (Map by Wayne Shishido)

Japanese bombers, shown here, attacked Corregidor on Komori's first morning there. As he described the scene in his journal, "hovering wings of death sprayed and bombed, and tore us apart."

US soldiers man anti-aircraft artillery, or ack-ack, on Corregidor.
(Courtesy of Olive-Drab.com)

General Douglas MacArthur declared Manila an "open city" on December 26, 1941.

Komori described having roast turkey for Christmas dinner on Corregidor after the G2's "nightmarish" evacuation from Manila on a small tugboat. The following morning they were attacked: "hovering wings of death sprayed and bombed, and tore us apart. Our ack-ack [anti-aircraft artillery] was far short, and our own ring of steel inadequate." With bombs blasting through their concrete barracks, the G2 team survived by taking shelter in a nearby water culvert. Having spent the day after Christmas being bombarded by Japanese fighter plane attacks, the G2 unit left Middle Side barracks in the center of Corregidor and made it to Bataan under cover of darkness on December 27.

Cleared of US troops, Manila was declared an open city on December 26. The designation of "open city" is a type of partial surrender, signaling that defensive measures have been halted, and is designed to protect civilians as well as historic landmarks. Once the declaration is made, the expectation is that opposing forces will cease destructive attacks and simply march into the city, leaving the remaining civilians and what is left of their city unharmed.

On January 1, 1942, the CIP, or Corps of Intelligence Police, became the CIC, or Counter Intelligence Corps. Counter intelligence involves, in addition to simply the collection of information, activities designed to prevent or thwart intelligence gathering by the enemy. While the CIC's own history of the division during the war notes that this

was a change in name only, the fact that they were at war
meant that the CIC was growing and taking on new and
varied duties at this time. The CIC force in the Philippines at
the time comprised six officers and fourteen agents. Komori
and Sakakida, the only two agents of Japanese ancestry,
were assigned to the regular army. Komori was attached to
G2 headquarters at the front under General Jonathan M.
Wainwright, MacArthur's Commander of the Philippine
Department and the senior commander in the field, and
Sakakida was assigned to work under Major Stuart Wood,
MacArthur's chief language officer. With this move, Komori
and Sakakida became the first CIC agents ever attached to
combat troops in battle. They were eventually joined by
Clarence Yamagata, a Hawaiʻi-born Nisei who had earned
a law degree in California and had been in the Philippines
working for the Japanese Consulate when war broke out.
Captain Raymond had convinced Yamagata to join them
following the evacuation of Manila, and Yamagata remained
in the intelligence service throughout the war.

The Manila Detachment of G2 set up its "Bamboo
Headquarters" in the jungles of Bataan with little precedent
to guide them. One particular job designated to Komori
by General Wainwright was identifying Japanese troops,
sometimes Kempeitai (the notorious military police branch of
the Japanese Imperial Army) who managed to pass through
army lines disguised as Filipino tribesmen, and closing the

General Jonathan M. Wainwright was MacArthur's senior commander in the Philippines. (Courtesy of the National Archives)

The notorious Kempeitai, a military police branch of the Japanese Army, were active in Manila during the Japanese occupation. (Courtesy of the Mainichi Newspaper Company)

loopholes and gaps in security that led to such breeches. Later in his life when he described this period, Komori wrote that, "as bad as war is, jungle warfare is worse." He recalled in a 1979 interview with *The Honolulu Advertiser* how scarce food was, and how he and the other agents resorted to eating army mules and horses, water buffalo, and monkeys. "Monkey tastes like turkey," Komori said, "but a skinned monkey looked like a child." Malnutrition and malaria took their toll on the troops, although Filipino scouts told Komori that he was spared from the disease because he ate monkey. Sleeping on the jungle floor, surrounded by pythons and lizards as well as relentless bombing, Komori took on many tasks unrelated to his specialized training as a CIC agent simply because there was no one else to do them. An account written by noted WWII historian Ian Sayer and author Douglas Botting that was entered into the Congressional Record in 1996 described this period:

> In Bataan they [Komori and Sakakida] operated from makeshift headquarters of bamboo sticks and banana leaves in a clearing in the jungle, where amid the screeching birds and clacking palms they plunged into a frenzy of activity. They went on patrols and scouting expeditions through the lines, interrogated prisoners-of-war, interned collaborators, collected enemy documents and translated them, amassed information of all kinds about Japanese movements and intentions.

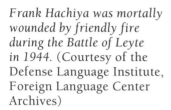

Frank Hachiya was mortally wounded by friendly fire during the Battle of Leyte in 1944. (Courtesy of the Defense Language Institute, Foreign Language Center Archives)

Komori wrote of this period that, "in the shifting battlelines of Bataan, it was a ticklish business, going up to the battlefields to identify corpses and gather information among the dead Japs. . . . Among the troops, I was constantly in danger of being shot for a Jap in disguise." Indeed, he told the *Honolulu Star Bulletin* in a 1944 interview that he was "surprised I wasn't shot at accidentally by our own men during those hectic days at Bataan and Corregidor." This was not an unreasonable fear. Later in the war, another Nisei, Frank Hachiya, was mortally wounded by friendly fire as he approached the American lines with documents that completely mapped out the Japanese army's defenses. He had acquired these documents after being air-dropped behind the lines, and despite being shot, crawled far enough to deliver them to an American officer.

Komori later wrote that in Bataan, he and his fellow agents started from scratch to build a security force. They took on many responsibilities, including observation and courier activity, patrolling and scouting, liaison with agents beyond enemy lines, safeguarding captured documents and POWs, internment and interrogation of POWs, and security of information along the lines of communication—a range of work that could not have been done by other army personnel. The makeshift group that included CIC, G2 (Intelligence), and civilian personnel were, in fact, carrying out a complete enemy identification service, a task now undertaken by many agencies, each contributing a particular skill set to the collaborative effort to achieve a similar result to that accomplished in the bamboo headquarters. Komori gave much of the credit for the group's productivity to Captain Raymond, whose inspiration it was to set Nisei agents to the task and whose faith in the Nisei never wavered.

Likewise, Komori's faith in and dedication to his leaders and to the US cause never wavered. While Captain Raymond was an important figure in Komori's life, both as a mentor and a friend, General MacArthur was, Komori felt, like "a God shaping my destiny." One day in Bataan, Komori wrote

General Douglas MacArthur (left) confers with Major General Sutherland in their make-shift offices in the Malinta Tunnel on Corregidor in March 1942. (Courtesy of the Naval History and Heritage Command)

that while he was translating a document, "MacArthur came along the trail and greeted me courteously as I stood aside for him to pass." Komori only managed a quick "Hello, sir," but knew that "the instant I stood in the shadow cast upon me by MacArthur on that trail in Bataan sealed my future destiny."

Indeed, Komori would remain personally loyal to MacArthur throughout his military career and his life. It is this loyalty and pride, rather than deprivation and hardship, that are highlighted in his own accounts of the war. In his poem "Golden Hearts of Men of Steel," written on Bataan in January 1942, Komori left a vivid example of the great pride he felt, not only in his mission, but in the men he worked with as well.

Golden Hearts of Men of Steel

On a Bataan hill,
We watched with hearts of gold.
We're sentinels of steel,
Reflecting colors bold,
The sunlight shining still,
On trees in mountains cold.

We glow in unison,
We scintillate for faith.
As beacons of the sun,
We brightly glisten forth,
Until the day is done
For us so close to earth.

Within our golden cores,
All of us bravely feel,
We should protect these shores,
And virgin wooded hills,
So rich in mineral ores,
Till liberty bells peal.

At night the Pleiades beam,
Up in a patch of heaven.
Like diamonds they gleam
As if by golden hearts given
Those sparks of hope. Those seem
Returned by Sisters Seven.

As the CIC agents grew more successful in acquiring enemy documents and equipment from the front lines, they encountered a new danger—the great collection of foreign materials became a risk in itself. In his memoirs, Komori recalled a day when Major Wood suddenly yelled, "Get those things out of here!" when it was discovered that amongst the soldier's letters, maps, and telegrams, a Molotov cocktail and a land mine had made their way into the makeshift headquarters. Yet, despite the danger, the materials recovered provided details about strategy, training, unit identification, morale, call signs, code names, and descriptions of ships previously unknown to US commanders. Particularly useful out of all the captured documents were the diaries kept by most Japanese soldiers. These invaluable discoveries were translated and compiled into reports destined for MacArthur's headquarters.

Because of the volume of work, a translation unit was eventually set up in Malinta Tunnel, the underground network of tunnels built by the US on Corregidor in 1932, which also served as a hospital, headquarters for the US Army, and for a time, headquarters for the government of the Philippine Commonwealth. Sayer and Botting described the conditions on Corregidor at the time:

> Back on Corregidor they found the Rock was not a nice place to be. It was now raked daily from dawn to dusk by Japanese air and artillery bombardment, so that the garrison was forced to seek permanent shelter in the tunnel system bored deep inside the hills, where they eked out an acutely uncomfortable troglodytic existence on half rations.

Work went on under cramped and difficult conditions inside Malinta Tunnel on Corregidor during the Battle of Bataan. (Courtesy of the National Archives)

The work in Malinta Tunnel involved translating captured documents and monitoring and analyzing all Japanese Air Force communications, which were broadcasting in the clear. Despite the initial assignment of Komori to the front and Sakakida to the language officer Major Wood, the sheer volume of material and the extreme shortage of personnel trained to undertake translation work, meant that both of them were sorely needed on Corregidor and Bataan. A routine was established whereby Komori and Sakakida alternated three-day shifts, often working up to twenty hours a day. When one was in Bataan the other was in Corregidor, an exhausting pattern they kept up for months.

Komori wrote in his personal journal that, "before the fall of Bataan everyone, I mean everyone, was supremely confident that help would be forthcoming soon. And in the meantime, we felt as I did when I penned the following in February 1942 in a little translation shack at night."

All

Somewhere far from home I stand,
Alive in all this glory.
Sentry post and staff-man's work,
As if it were a story.

Reams they write of hero stuff,
Of how a battle rages.
Proud am I to own that now,
I live within those pages.

Pretty soon we'll all bed down,
To rest in all this foliage.
Crickets chirping in the trees,
And radio sounding homage.

Far be it for us to say,
How long we'll be defending.
But, we don't mind it at all,
For ours won't shirk in sending.

What has passed we must forget.
It is the future sweetness,
Calling us to do our best,
No matter who the witness.

We can live by unity,
Deprived of all the pleasures,
By devotion, leadership,
And all the noble treasures.

For a time, the men were bolstered by their confidence, but by March 1942, it was clear that help would not be coming. Having been on the defensive since the attack at Pearl Harbor, which was followed by attacks on Manila and Guam, and because of Washington's Europe-first policy, the US military was still playing catch-up in the Pacific. Allies of the United States also had their hands full in 1942 trying, but failing, to forestall the fall of the Dutch Indies, Hong Kong, Malaya, Singapore, and Burma. And so, "after three months of bitter and intensive combat, malnutrition, and disease," Sayer and Botting explained, "the men were

American troops emerge from Malinta Tunnel as the US Army surrendered to Japan in April 1942. (Courtesy of the National Archives)

exhausted. By now the daily food intake was down to 800 calories per man; and 90 percent of the Filipino army had no shoes." With surrender imminent, it was time for headquarters to revise the plan for US forces on the Bataan Peninsula and Corregidor.

General MacArthur left Bataan for Australia on March 21, 1942, to establish his new headquarters in Melbourne. (MacArthur's general headquarters (GHQ) was moved to Brisbane, Australia's northernmost city in July 1942 and remained there until November 1944.) In the midst of the evacuation, both General MacArthur and General Wainwright expressed deep concern for the safety of Komori and Sakakida. These two CIC agents would fare worse under captivity than Caucasian troops since Japan refused to recognize the right of anyone of Japanese ancestry to swear allegiance to another country. The roles they had played, first as spies in pre-war Manila and then as CIC agents in the US Army, would be considered treasonous, and punishable by death if they were captured.

On April 8, Komori was rushed to Bataan's Mariveles Harbor on orders from former Captain, now Major, Raymond, who was intent on protecting the safety of his protégé. From there, he sailed for Corregidor, but halfway across the channel, the vessel he was in came under heavy fire. Eventually, they made it to port and then to the relative safety of Malinta Tunnel. Barraged by Japanese General Homma Masaharu's forces, Bataan fell the next morning.

Approximately 12,000 stranded US troops and 63,000 Filipinos were captured and forced on a six-day march to Balanga, the capital of Bataan, a journey that would come to be known as the Bataan Death March. Because of Major Raymond's insistence on removing him, Komori was spared this fate. Raymond himself never made it to safety—he is believed to have died on a Japanese ship filled with American POWs that was sunk by American torpedoes.

The Philippine Islands were, at this point, almost completely under Japanese control; Corregidor was one of the last Allied holdouts in the country. As conditions continued to deteriorate on Corregidor, plans were made to evacuate both Komori and Sakakida to Australia where they would join General MacArthur. Sakakida bravely gave up his spot to Yamagata, realizing that his particular history as a civilian working for the Japanese Consulate in Manila who had left to work for the US Army would put him and his family in grave danger. This left Komori as the only CIC agent authorized for an escape to Australia. On April 13, 1942, Komori, Yamagata, and Colonel Chih Wang, an emissary for the Chinese military leader Chiang Kai-shek, were taken to the airstrip on Corregidor. In what General Wainwright called a fifty-fifty proposition, they were flown by pilot Bill Bradford to Iloilo, Panay Island, in an army trainer that had previously crash-landed while bringing in medical supplies. This plane accounted for one-third of the US fleet in the Philippines at the time. Komori "talked fast to get in the front seat" when he learned that they were to leave in a dual-control bi-plane, "for I was going to use my flight training to save myself." In the journal he kept at the time, Komori described the little four-seater plane's three o'clock a.m. takeoff:

> Bill whooped as we forced our plane into the air, after bouncing up 50 feet as our sputtering engine warmed-up after the searchlight turned on too quickly for sufficient warm-up on the ground. We finally were on the way out to freedom, flying over dark, unfriendly Manila Bay. Bill cautioned me to watch out for signal lights on the ground, and allowed me flight control of our craft, "a bamboo fleet," while he studied his map with a flash-light. Towards morning, we flew low over Panay rice-fields trying to locate the camouflaged rice-field airport. And we suddenly zoomed into it, after failing to see the signal flares since daylight had dimmed the lights. The rice stalks opened up into a converted hangar & closed behind us.

He also described the escape in a 1944 interview with the *Honolulu Star Bulletin*, where he added the detail that "the airstrip was a rock beach and we were lucky to get the plane off the ground. I guess we would have crashed if the plane hadn't hit a rock which bumped the plane about 50 feet into the air to help in the takeoff."

And yet, on the night, Major General Chih Wang, Clarence Yamagata, ~~majority~~ I, and Bill Bradford were sent off by Major Dooley, aide to Wainwright, with the plane co-piloted by me. Bill whooped as we forced our plane into the air, after bouncing up 50 feet as our sputtering engine warmed-up after the searchlight turned on too quickly for sufficient warm-up on the ground. We finally were on the way out to freedom, flying over dark unfriendly Manila Bay. Bill cautioned me to watch out for signal lights on the ground, and often allowed me flight control

The Flight From Panay (Iloilo Golf Club). 13 April, about 2:00 p.m.

our craft, "a bamboo fleet" while he studied his map with a flashlight. Towards morning we flew low over Panay rice-fields trying to locate the camouflaged rice field air port. And we suddenly zoomed into it, after failing to see the signal flares since daylight had dimmed the lights. The rice stalks opened-up into a converted hangar & closed behind us.

These pages from Arthur Komori's personal journal show his description of his harrowing escape from Corregidor.

*Pappy Gunn and Arthur Komori (not pictured) first met at the KT Flying
School in Honolulu.* (Courtesy of Nathaniel Gunn)

From Panay, they flew farther south to Del Monte
Field on Mindanao Island, also in the Philippines, on a
B-25 Mitchell with legendary Army Air Corps pilot Paul I.
"Pappy" Gunn at the controls. Coincidentally, Gunn was
a former employee of K-T Flying Services, Komori's flight
school in Honolulu. Komori later described the flight in
detail: "Captain 'P. I.' Gunn rescued us from Panay with
his B-25 in a flight through broad daylight through enemy

territory in a hedge-hopping, canyon-shooting, wave-skipping trip, which were Gunn's specialties." They survived "in broad daylight through enemy territory" by "flying only a few feet above our own shadow" to avoid detection.

Having arrived at Del Monte, Komori and the rest of the crew shared a meal at General William F. Sharpe's table. They soon realized, however, that they had been discovered, and would have to make another daring escape. Komori later wrote that he could "never forget the rings of fire around the air strips that night, for the Japs finally found that secret base."

The next leg of their escape was a seventeen-hour flight through enemy territory to Darwin, Australia in a modified B-25 bomber, a flight that set a record for the longest flight that type of aircraft had ever made. Komori remained convinced for the rest of his life that this flight had been a "test hop" to prove that the B-25 could make the distance, because raids on Japan using B-25s launched from the aircraft carrier USS *Hornet* began just a few days later. From Darwin, they flew on to Melbourne where Komori joined General MacArthur's staff. By April 16, after three days of traveling, Komori had reached his destination and his home for the foreseeable future. Immediate danger was now behind them, and Komori later commemorated the relative peace of Melbourne with this poem, written on June 14, 1942.

Bombing raids on Japan using B-25s launched from the aircraft carrier USS Hornet *began in April 1942.* (Courtesy of the National Museum of the US Air Force)

The Austral Prayer

Tonight, I look upon Australia
As haven not yet burst asunder by
The dogs of war. A pink Camelia,
Whose beauty hounds of war can never buy.
Its cities, desert, ocean, bush, and land
Are solid with potentialities.
Inviolable and sacredly they stand,
As shrine to those brave personalities,
Who fought and died so this great land may live.
Will there be deadly thrusts of enemies,
Or doves of peace and branches of olive?
Oh God, must there be all these infamies?
We pray for peace in heaven and on earth,
From Milky Way, to Libya and Perth.

CHAPTER 3

In War and Peace

B-25s lined up on the deck of the USS Hornet. (Courtesy of the National Museum of the US Air Force)

So great was the need for secrecy in the escape from Corregidor that not even the War Department in Washington, DC, could account for Arthur Komori's whereabouts after April 1942. Komori had received a confidential letter from General Wainwright, also sent to the detachment headquarters of the US Forces in the Philippines,

officially relieving him of his assignment in the Philippines
and reassigning him to the US forces under Major General
Charles A. Willoughby in Australia. Despite this official
notification, the army reported him missing in action on
May 7, almost a month after his departure from Corregidor.
(A letter notifying his family of his missing status was sent a full
nineteen months later, in December 1943.)

While the larger bureaucracy of the army may have lost
track of him, Komori's immediate superiors knew exactly where
he was and how valuable his contribution in the Philippines
had been. Soon after arriving in Australia, in June 1942, Major
General Willoughby submitted a recommendation that Komori
be awarded the Purple Heart. In his recommendation,
Willoughby wrote that Staff Sergeant Komori

> merits this award in recognition for his services on
> Bataan, as a member of that very small group of
> Japanese interpreters, one officer and five men, who
> handled identification of enemy units successfully
> during the entire Philippine campaign.

He further noted that Komori "made frequent trips to the
active front lines to interrogate prisoners of war and arrange
for the delivery of captured enemy equipment and documents
at great personal hazard," and that "his Japanese ancestry
exposed him to certain death in case of capture." Despite this
glowing recommendation, the Purple Heart was denied because
by the time the recommendation was received, the award was

only being granted to the wounded. The notification of this rejection noted that, "unless Sergeant Komori's action can be considered as 'gallantry in action' and a Silver Star awarded, I do not see that any award can be made." Willoughby's subsequent recommendation of Komori to receive the Silver Star for "gallantry in action" was also denied because official records did not show any examples in Komori's history. The response included the comment that the "records do not show how [Komori] happens to be at G2 [in Australia]. . . apparently under an arrangement agreed upon by Major General Willoughby and Colonel [Elliott R.] Thorpe."

In the absence of official recognition, a token of appreciation was given in January 1943, when Colonel Evans, Chief of the Southwest Pacific Branch, submitted a memo of commendation to be placed in the files of both Arthur Komori and Richard Sakakida for their undercover work in Manila prior to the war. In the memo, Colonel Evans noted that,

> these two non-commissioned officers, both Nisei (Hawaiian-born Japanese with American citizenship) were assigned to and undertook duty of greatest importance in the Philippine Department under my command during the period in 1941, ending with the outbreak of the war. They performed this duty in a highly satisfactory manner, with complete disregard of the personal danger in which they found themselves.

This recognition, however, was simply a memo to be placed in their files, not a recommendation for an award.

Komori had not been in Australia long before he realized that the CIC in general seemed to have fallen through the administrative cracks, just like him. He wrote in a 1945 memo that in April 1942 he had been the only CIC agent to escape from Bataan, and that having arrived in Melbourne, he found "little evidence of any CIC unit, and I was puzzled by the lack of recognition of such a unit." The memo described his being questioned satirically, being told that his status was not known, and feeling that his work was not being recognized. He added, "bearing in mind the little recognition CIC had in Bataan, I was out to give it all the recognition it deserved." But a few lines later he wrote that, having spoken openly of his CIC training and work to staff at GHQ, he was "severely reprimanded" by Colonel Thorpe "for not consulting him first." This account of Komori's transition from battle to CIC work at GHQ illustrates the difficult nature of the life of a CIC agent. One reason for this had to do with the secretive nature of the CIC, but in Komori's case, his ethnicity added another layer of strain to the mix.

The very nature of CIC work meant that it went largely unrecognized by most of the regular army personnel. One of the ways this secrecy manifested itself was in the handling of rank within the CIC. The CIC School, in their publication *The History of the CIC in WWII*, described the issue in a section they titled "The Problem of Rank":

> The rank of the agent was at best a partial secret within the army. Counter Intelligence Corps men were instructed to conceal their actual rank by using the term "agent" or "special agent." Concealment of rank in the zone of the interior was not too great a problem since agents worked in civilian clothes. The average civilian respected Counter Intelligence Corps credentials and was not concerned with the actual rank of the bearer.
>
> When his mission was changed from the zone of the interior to foreign theaters of operations, the Counter Intelligence Corps agent, in some cases, wore the military uniform indicating his status. This factor was a disadvantage in dealing with officers of the United States Army and officers of the Allied Forces. The low rank of the leaders of some detachments often had a hampering effect, especially in their relationships with allied services in the theaters and with coordinate agencies in the United States.

This was not an issue within the CIC itself. The same history notes that, "in spite of the fact that most of these men worked as corporals or sergeants, the organization obtained outstanding men." But it was an issue when working with other branches of service whose members were unfamiliar with the CIC and their mission. Komori mentions specifically an incident involving the rank issue when a circular was distributed indicating that all CIC agents should realize firstly that they were enlisted men and should act accordingly. This attitude resulted, in two particular instances Komori described, in no provisions for the quartering of CIC agents with officers and in attempts to restrict CIC agents from moving freely about the Northwest Territory (of Australia), both cases described by him as presenting unnecessary obstacles that made it harder for him to do his job.

Yet he "realized strongly" that officers not having had CIC training did not appreciate CIC activities or principles. And knowing this, Komori carried on proudly and to the best of his ability, still completely dedicated both to the CIC and to his original goal of proving himself. In fact, for the most part, Komori did not mind this situation. A true CIC man, he was happy to serve in silence. He was assigned to Major General Willoughby's G2 unit upon his arrival in Australia, and from this time until the end of the war, Komori's role might best be described as that of a "utility player," working wherever and whenever he was needed. One of his first tasks was to write a report on the methods of interrogation he and Sakakida had developed when dealing with Japanese POWs in Manila and Bataan. This "kindness and understanding" approach, playing to the solders' sense of honor, became "the definitive American guideline" for the interrogation of Japanese POWs and paid dividends in both blood and treasure in the degree to which it shortened the war. As Komori described the situation,

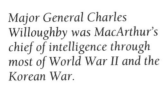

Major General Charles Willoughby was MacArthur's chief of intelligence through most of World War II and the Korean War.

warfare against the Japanese in the jungle was something new in our Army then, so we began laying the groundwork for intelligence operations against the enemy by consolidating our experience in the Battles of Bataan and Corregidor at GHQ. . . . I was able to write various reports on the operations of a CIC unit in combat, which were highly considered by Major General Willoughby.

Once this was done, Komori had an interlude of calm in what had thus far been a very busy career. With no immediate outlet for his talents, he was given work as a driver. The army provided a generous per diem that allowed him to live in hotels, a sharp contrast to the jungles of Bataan. But with his countrymen "slogging it out in the mud," Komori chaffed against this luxurious, idle lifestyle. He was anxious to make further contributions to the war effort.

Fortunately for him, this interlude was short-lived. By December 1942 the US Army in Australia would comprise 300,000 troops and another 50,000 civilian employees, and the CIC would be responsible for protecting this entire operation from espionage and subversion. Within weeks, Komori began his work in the investigation of internal affairs. Many years later, he described this line of work in his memoirs:

> From April to August in 1942, and from December 1942 to August in 1943, I was continually in the hair, so to speak, of USAFIA [United States Army Forces in Australia] and USASOS [United States Army Services of Supply] headquarters officers and men with my security and loyalty investigation.

In addition to researching and giving lectures on Japanese intelligence and military capabilities, Komori was also responsible for sealing security leaks, investigating "crypto signal" personnel, conducting internal security surveys, and vetting both American and Australian employees.

In between these security investigations, from September to December 1942, Komori was assigned to help create a new, centralized US and Australian intelligence unit called the Allied Translator and Interpreter Section (ATIS) in Indooroopilly, Brisbane. The Military Intelligence Service Language School (MISLS) had opened on July 1, 1942, in

an airfield hangar at the Presidio in San Francisco and had
soon become one of the most important centers for army
intelligence during the war.

The first group of linguists, about fifty in number and
predominantly Nisei, arrived in Melbourne in September 1942
to translate captured enemy documents. Komori, delegated
to be ATIS's non-commissioned officer (NCO), was placed
in charge of these new arrivals. He took his contingent to
Brisbane, "and we set-up a closely barricaded stockade where
allied officers and men worked day and night in pouring over
materials captured in Guadalcanal, and later New Guinea." In
an interview he gave to the Kauaʻi Museum in 1992, Komori
described the early days of ATIS: Marines had recently landed
in the Solomon Islands, which had been occupied by the
Japanese, and were sending a steady stream of documents
and POWs to Brisbane, where he and his team set to work
translating, interrogating, and reporting their findings to
Lieutenant Colonel Sidney Mashbir, the Commandant of ATIS.
The linguists worked tirelessly "all together in one compound
with barbed wire" surrounding them, a necessary precaution
due to the amount of classified material they handled.

Although Komori didn't particularly enjoy life in
"Brisbane town," as he called it, he certainly was proud of the
work he did there and of the collaborative nature of ATIS,
calling it "a great allied and inter-service organization." It
wasn't just a US installment in Australia; rather, it was a

joint effort between the countries to help bring the war to a close as soon as possible. It was also largely populated by Nisei servicemen like Komori, and this fact finally brought some relief from the sense of isolation he had felt ever since his recruitment. The formation of ATIS coincided with the relocation of 120,000 Japanese Americans into internment camps and the discharge and designation as 4C, or "enemy alien," of hundreds of Nisei soldiers, formerly members of the Hawai'i Territorial Guard. But far away in Australia, this first group of fifty Nisei linguists, a number that would swell to six thousand before the end of the war, were given their own opportunity to prove themselves, and Komori was proud, both of them and of his role in helping to shape ATIS. Later in his life, Komori recalled his sentiments at the time:

> During the war, when a pall of suspicion lay over all of Japanese blood, the American-Japanese sought to justly assert themselves, making a supreme effort to rise up from their little Tokyos and Osakas of Hawaii and California and going to war against their relatives in Japan. I am thankful that they too cast-off the alien yoke of their parents. Perhaps, not as radically as I had done, but nevertheless with the same clear-sighted objective of proving their Americanism. With their added participation, in the middle stages of the war, I no longer felt as one among thousands, and felt no longer as a freak or target for curious eyes on the battle front.

What their presence did not relieve, however, was the ongoing suspicion of Japanese Americans, since the secretive nature of their work did nothing to help Komori's fellow troops understand his role or that of the other Nisei who were making their contribution to the US war effort. Joseph Harrington, in his book *Yankee Samurai*, refers to the Americans of Japanese ancestry wielding "the secret weapon of language." Similarly, the MIS Association of Northern California, in its history of the war, notes that, "the vital role of Nisei linguists in the successful combat strategy of the American forces was generally concealed from the Japanese." They described General MacArthur's wish to keep this advantage, a strategy that resulted in the MIS Nisei being almost totally absent from the press information and pictorial record of the Pacific War.

Major General Willoughby would later claim that the work of the Nisei translators in ATIS shortened the war by several years. This sentiment was echoed by Colonel Mashbir in his book, *I Was an American Spy*, where he wrote that "had it not been for the loyalty, fidelity, patriotism, and ability of these American Nisei, that part of the war in the Pacific which was dependent upon intelligence gleaned from captured documents and prisoners of war would have been a far more hazardous, long drawn-out affair." A history of the CIC in World War II published by the CIC School in 1951 reinforces this impression, referring to the Allied Translator and Interpreter Section as possibly the most important single intelligence agency of the Pacific theater of the war, but adding that it was also possibly the most secret.

Even though Komori had helped to set up ATIS and had done much translation work himself, he remained principally a CIC agent. His concern at ATIS, rather than serving as a translator himself, was to organize the new translation and interpretation unit so that the overwhelming amount of material coming in from the battlefields could be used to the Allies' advantage. Because of this larger role, Komori did not stay within the barbed wire barricades of ATIS for long. As Komori told the Kaua'i Museum, "our [the CIC] assignment

The number of translators working at ATIS swelled to 6,000 by the end of the war. This photograph is in keeping with their status as a "secret weapon," showing only their backs so they could not be recognized by the enemy.

Komori traveled to the Australian Outback where he trained Aborigines, shown here, to rescue and care for downed Allied pilots. (Courtesy of the National Library of Australia)

was not only spying, but the security of our forces." As part of this work, Komori left Brisbane for the Australian outback where he made contact with Aborigines in the Arnhem Land region north of Darwin. Komori taught the Aborigines to locate and rescue pilots who had crash-landed after bombing missions in Java and New Guinea, exchanging gifts for their cooperation. He later wrote about the fantastic wildlife he saw in the Northern Territory: "buffalos, snakes, crocodiles (seagoing), burramondie (fish), emus, cranes (dancing), lizards, kangaroos, wallabys, ant hills, etc." He experienced "the strange dances of the 'corroberee,' and heard the eerie music of the 'didgeridoo' by night, and spear and boomerang throwing by the natives by day."

He also added, in an entry that, ironically, demonstrated some of the prejudice that he himself had experienced but that was commonly accepted at the time, that "the colored cave paintings and burial places were ghostly reminders of the witch-craft and cannibalism of these once great dirty brown people."

Throughout 1943, while the services provided by ATIS proved essential to success in the Pacific, Komori moved on to other assignments, among them, finally receiving his first formal training in security and counterintelligence, although by this time, with his experience, he often occupied the dual role of student and teacher. He was one of two Americans to attend Field Security Section (FSS) School in Brisbane in January 1943 for two weeks of field security courses where, in addition to taking the course, he "lectured on Japanese intelligence." Later that year, in September, he attended CIC School in Brisbane, again for a two-week course for special agents.

By December the army had expanded its language training school, but the evacuation of Japanese Americans from the West Coast had forced its relocation to Camp Savage in Minnesota. Komori was sent to Camp Savage for two months where, again, he played the dual role of instructor and student. He later wrote that, "General Willoughby wanted me to go to Camp Savage, Minnesota, and teach the Nisei studying in the MIS Language School of battle conditions and situations." In another interview, he said that, "from 7 December 1943 to 7 February 1944 I was a student at the Military Intelligence Language School, Camp Savage, Minnesota," noting that since he was only on a 60-day temporary duty assignment (TDY) from the SWPA (Southwest Pacific Area), he did not have time to complete the nine-month course.

Three Hawai'i-born Nisei play in the snow during their training at Camp Savage in Minnesota. (Courtesy of Takejiro Higa)

The purpose of this assignment was largely educational, of course, but it also seems to have been meant to be something of a vacation, granted in return for his exemplary service. Komori's journals refer to Major General Willoughby's orders that he stop in Hawai'i to visit family on the way both to and from Minnesota, and that he get plenty of rest during his time at Camp Savage. Never one to shirk his duties, Komori seems to have followed this order to the letter, referring to his visit home as "a grand reunion with my family and friends." This was the first time his family had seen him since his abrupt departure three years earlier and the first real communication after three years of silence.

Komori's personal account of the two months at Camp Savage has an air of relaxation about it as well. He left few details in his writings about the classes he took or lectures he gave, noting only how genuinely pleased he was that he had been "able to inspire the students with a firsthand account of our battle of linguists and words." He added that "it gave the students great insight and inspiration because my appearance representing the Allied Headquarters gave them first-hand proof of the reception they would have—with open arms by the Allied troops and commanders," a far cry from the racism and segregation many Nisei faced in the United States.

In February 1944, Komori left Camp Savage, following his first white Christmas, and flew once again to Hawai'i. On this leg of the journey, he gave an interview to the *Honolulu Star-Bulletin*'s Lawrence Nakatsuka, whom he told, for the first time, the epic story of the Battle of Bataan from the point of view of a native-born Hawai'i resident. Although he intentionally "forgot to mention CIC in that or any later newspaper report," for security reasons, the newspaper was not allowed to publish his story at that time. Upon his return to Australia, Komori reported the prohibition to Major General Willoughby, who wrote to Hawaiian G2 headquarters, requesting that the story be released. It was published in two parts on April 17 and 18, 1944, and for the first time Hawai'i residents were treated to a first-hand account of the horrors of jungle warfare in the Philippines and the harrowing escape in broken-down planes through constant enemy bombardment. Komori knew the article would be well received, "much to the happiness of the suspect Japanese Americans in Hawaii." For most of them, this would have been the first news of him since the rumors of a pilot shot down over Pearl Harbor wearing a Japanese uniform and a McKinley High School class ring.

Back in Australia in April 1944, Komori became a liaison to the Australian government. He was assigned to the Department of Information in Melbourne, where his duties consisted of monitoring, translating, and evaluating Japanese broadcasts. He wrote that, "it was as if I sat in the dress-circle of war, for I visualized the troops of the Mikado reeling back in Burma, China, New Guinea, and the Philippines." An analyst

6—*Honolulu Star-Bulletin, Monday, April 17, 1944*

Only Hawaii Survivor of Bataan Tells Story of 11th Hour Escape

By LAWRENCE NAKATSUKA

(In this exclusive interview, Sergeant Arthur Komori of Honolulu relates his experiences during the epic of Bataan, his 11th hour evacuation to Corregidor by orders of Gen. Douglas MacArthur and, finally, his hazardous 2,000 mile flight by air to Australia. The story, which has been cleared by army authorities, is published in two installments.)

Two years after the epic of Bataan, the story can now be told of the only Hawaiian born soldier of the United States army known to have escaped from the Philippines after the enemy's invasion.

* * *

The graphic tale of his 11th hour escape from Japanese captors was related to The Star-Bulletin by the survivor, Technical Sergeant Arthur Komori of Honolulu.

* * *

The stocky, 28 year old Maui born soldier lived through three months of jungle hell on Bataan, then was ordered evacuated to Corregidor the day before the battered peninsula fell.

After five days on the Rock, he was flown out to Australia and safety, 2,000 miles away.

Sergeant Komori stopped in Honolulu, his home town before the war, while en route to the south Pacific for active duty again, after two months of temporary mainland duty.

With some reluctance, "like talking about a bad dream," the sergeant narrated his story:

* * *

"I am a 'nisei'—an American of Japanese ancestry — and you know what the Japs would have done to me if they caught someone of their own race fighting against them on Bataan.

* * *

Sgt. Komori

and Filipino defenders in the jungles on that peninsula.

* * *

"At first, we had some army chow which wasn't so bad but later we had only rice and gravy for a month.

"When tomatoes and pickles ran out, we had to boil young tree leaves as substitute for greens. For meat we hunted monkeys.

"I didn't eat monkey meat at first, but one day when I got really hungry and saw it being broiled over a fire—it smelled awfully good—I ate some of it. It tasted like roast turkey and reminded me of the turkey dinner I had on Corregidor on Christmas Day.

* * *

"We also had mule meat, horse

The Honolulu Star-Bulletin *published this interview with Arthur Komori, in which he described his experiences in the Battle of Bataan, in April 1944 after several months delay.* (Courtesy of the *Honolulu Star Advertiser*) from the Melbourne Law School extracted political, economic, and domestic details of life in Japan from these evaluations, and Komori took pride in finding his words, complete with American verbiage, in the morning papers. In this position, he uncovered information about Japan's lack of skilled pilots and depleted war materials. He even uncovered information about operations of the American Navy, often from speeches made by high-ranking Japanese officials like Prime Minister Hideki Tōjō and Admiral Mitsumasa Yonai. As Komori put it, "[i]t tickled us every time the Jap broadcasters screamed and ranted in rage, for... the more they screamed the greater were their losses."

During that year on loan to the Australian government, Komori worked at night on his monitoring and translation duties, and during the day, he could be found courting Marie N. Poon, an Australian Chinese woman whom he had first met in 1942. Later that year, he requested, and eventually received, permission to marry her, although it wasn't a simple process. The request was made to his commanding officer, Major General Thorpe, who denied him permission to marry. He later wrote that he had chosen his allegiance to the United States, and if a connection to Marie would jeopardize his ability to serve his country, he was "willing to think the matter over." But in the end, he called on his close association with Major General Willoughby to get permission—one of only two times he ever "pulled rank."

Many years later, Komori wrote of that period, "On per diem of $4 a day in Melbourne with my Australian bride. What a duty!" And yet, the country was still at war, and as he intercepted broadcasts that pointed to the impending defeat of the Japanese, he became increasingly "eager to set foot on free Philippines again." He had never forgotten about his fellow CIC agents that had been left behind in the Philippines, and as he told his wife, who was pregnant by this time, "the sooner I went north, the sooner I could go home and call for her from Honolulu." Having made these wishes widely known, Komori was ordered to join Major General Thorpe in Manila in March 1945. He flew into Manila on April 6, a week shy of three years since his escape, and later wrote that he had "never felt better in my life" than when he flew over Bataan and Corregidor, a bay full of sunken Japanese ships below him.

Once back in Manila, Komori rejoined the CIC where he had two goals. The first was to be part of the intelligence team as MacArthur prepared for the invasion of the Japanese home-land. The second, he wrote later, was to do as much as he could for the agents that had been lost and left behind three years prior. "I owed it," he said, "to my fellow CIC agents captured or hiding in the hills with guerillas, to search for them, or speak for them, since identification problems always existed with agents who had been in civilian clothes prior to the war."

Once again, the undercover nature of the CIC meant that Komori had to be content to work in the background, often

General MacArthur, shown wading ashore at Palo Beach on the island of Leyte, retook the Philippines in October 1944. (Courtesy of the National Archives)

When Komori returned to the Philippines in March 1945, he noted in his journal that Manila Bay was full of sunken Japanese ships. (Courtesy of the Harry S. Truman Library)

without recognition. As he recorded in his 1945 memo, "Upon my assignment to work, no typewriters, desks, and chairs were made available to Sgt. [Hisashi "Johnny"] Masuda and myself. No provisions were taken for equipping me with a side arm. Lt. Shelton and Lt. Col. Hoover were not even aware of my CIC status; the former telling me to wear stripes and the latter associating me as a member of the G-2 Evaluation Section."

And yet, there was work to be done, and Komori, along with his partner and fellow CIC agents threw themselves into their work, doing whatever needed to be done. Komori later described how in those weeks prior to Japan's surrender, the 493rd CIC detachment, to which he was now attached, "operated like a posse on jeeps, and no doubt, struck terror into the hearts of all collaborators… gaining the notoriety akin to that of the Gestapo or the Kempeitai." Komori was not entirely comfortable with this new face of the CIC, appearing "more like a gendarmaris or provost squad than the original 'silent service,'" but went on to say that "as all culprits apprehended by us will admit, we were never cruel, inhuman, or sadistic." Rather, in this, they

> tended to prove the versatility and flexibility of the CIC in pursuing its assigned military missions, whether in [a] defense zone such as Bataan, static zone in Australia, combat zone in New Guinea, or occupation zone in the Philippines and Japan.

With his new partner, California-born Sergeant Hisashi "Johnny" Masuda, Komori searched for and interrogated many Japanese spies in re-occupied Manila. At this point, spies were infiltrating Manila intent on "sabotage, assassination of our leaders, and other subversive activities." The benevolent approach again garnered excellent results, as he and Masuda obtained many confessions, allowing them what he called "the chance of a life-time to 'hang' Jap spies" in court. One spy's confession in particular, he remembered obtaining with a strange thrill.

> He proved cagey at first, but I brought all my techniques of interrogation into bearing and found him out. He gave the strangest, yet plausible reason (for a Jap) for confessing. He had been fearful of being tortured, and when instead he was not, and underwent instead a patient grilling and kind treatment, he was extremely grateful.

Komori also got the chance to accomplish his second goal—to speak for his fellow CIC agents. On April 7, he got a call from Major General Willoughby's secretary asking him for a full report on Technical Sergeant Sakakida.

Richard Sakakida, who had traveled from Hawai'i to Manila with Komori in March 1941, had been captured by the Japanese after the fall of the Philippines and imprisoned. In his account, he tells of the torture he suffered from the Japanese police. Through it, he maintained that he was a US civilian and

Richard Sakakida was recruited into the CIP with Komori in Honolulu in 1941.

was eventually put to work as an office lackey and houseboy for the Chief Judge Advocate of the 14th Japanese army headquarters. As the Japanese position became desperate, he was able to escape. After a long struggle through the jungle, he stumbled across US troops in mid-September 1945, wounded, wracked with disease, and unaware that the war was over. He convinced nearby US soldiers to bring him to their commanding officer, where he identified himself to a Major who was suspicious, but called the Field Office anyway. CIC agents came to collect him almost immediately, and Sakakida's return was celebrated with a banquet.

Although Komori was in Japan by the time Sakakida returned, he was overjoyed at the news that his fellow agent was safe. Komori said at the time that Sakakida's "successful duping of the Japs is the finest story of counter intelligence within enemy lines." He added that Sakakida's recovery was seen as more important even than the capture of General Yamashita. However, Sakakida had been off the grid and incommunicado for over two years. His story was questioned and his loyalty suspect. The testimony supporting Sakakida's loyalty Komori had given on April 7, five months before Sakakida emerged from the jungle, became a vital piece of the investigation. Major General Willoughby had asked Komori to report on the trustworthiness of the missing Nisei and in this case, his report helped to reinstate Sakakida's good name.

It is worth noting here that the internment of over 100,000 Japanese Americans in relocation camps had only ended earlier that year when the Supreme Court rescinded the Exclusion Order of 1942. The anti-Japanese sentiment would not fade away for some time, and yet, in the midst of all this, the word of one Nisei was quietly trusted to play a major part in determining the patriotism of another.

This photo of the Manzanar War Relocation Center in Central California is part of a series by Ansel Adams. (Courtesy of the Library of Congress)

Despite the many US victories that indicated the end of the war was near, Komori's time with the CIC in Manila went on for five months. Finally, on August 15, 1945, Emperor Hirohito himself announced Japan's surrender. In Manila, raucous celebrations and wild rejoicing filled the night. Komori wrote, "the liquor fumes and '4th of July' gun-smoke no doubt went to our heads, and we already imagined ourselves at home." Within a week, however, he was preparing for his next assignment—to serve as a translator for Major General Thorpe at the surrender ceremonies.

The days leading up to the formal surrender ceremonies were filled with emotion for the 30-year-old Komori, and his journal includes this poignant entry:

> The day for victory loomed suddenly after atomic bombs rained on Hiroshima and Nagasaki. There was wild rejoicing at our home that night. On the anniversary of my birth, 25 August 1945, I boarded the USN Transport *Sturgis,* bound for Tokyo Bay to keep a rendezvous with the surrendering Japs. As I rode out into Manila Bay on 26 August, my heart was filled with strange exultation.

He also composed this poem on board the *Sturgis* as they left Manila Bay.

Victory March

A day of many memories,
The day we passed Bataan;
And I stood watching sceneries,
Reflected by the red sun.

The thunder-head stood up on right,
With low clouds scudding past her.
The green on shore-line was a sight;
And shades of blue-black deeper,

Reminded me of camps of men,
In misty inland battles;
And high above the jungle fen,
Lay peaks of Mariveles.

Her razor ridges knifing up,
In sharp defiance always.
It stilled my over-flowing cup,
To see her on the slip-ways,

As mighty as a carrier.
Corregidor as escort,
Quiet as sleeping warrior,
But potent as a sea-fort.

We're on our way to Tokio,
To right the wrong of Death March.
We'll act as brave Boccaccio,
And build a victory arch.

It'll be a pretty masterpiece,
Bedecked with freedom's flowers,
A souvenir for lasting peace,
And blessed by all the Powers.

So as this transport surges on,
To meet the great Missouri,
I'll think of gallant Lexington,
And raging fights of Shuri;

And glory in the thought that we,
Are riding in to finish,

The demon reign of Japs on sea,
Till all their greed doth vanish.

Pearl Harbor and Manila Bays,
And all her fighting ladies,
To you our cheers and victory leis,
And all our lovely ladies.

28 August 1945

Aboard the US Naval transport
Sturgis *en route to Tokyo Bay*

On August 29th, two days before arriving in Tokyo Bay, Komori received word that his daughter, Rosemary, had been born. He was now "proudly father and hubby," eager both to return home and to stay and witness the historic moment close at hand. Two days later, Komori made this entry in his journal:

As we steamed steadily into Tokyo Bay on 31 August 1945, we saw our powerful armada in full line-up and huge B-29s winging overhead. Still the knowledge that the treaty of surrender was still to be signed kept us on edge. We wondered about the mysterious land of the Rising Sun and wondered what the people ashore must be thinking of at the sight of us.

On September 2, Komori watched from an escort boat as the Japanese surrendered to General MacArthur, Supreme Commander of the Allied Powers. The next day,

September 3, Komori stepped onto Japanese soil for the first time. He was the only CIC agent assigned to enter Japan with the first shipload of troops. There he acted as the personal interpreter for Major General Thorpe, Chief of CIC; Colonel Jennis Galloway, Commanding Officer for the 441st CIC Detachment; and Colonel Hoover, Chief Censor. Of this first excursion into Tokyo, Komori recorded these thoughts:

> It was with mixed feelings that we entered without any escort of any kind to guard our scouting trip around the city. We were the only Americans apparently, for we saw no other troops. The lack of any demonstrations, disorder, or even the slightest look of spite or hate cast in our direction was remarkable for a people who had been so bitterly fighting us. I, myself, thought it dangerous to invade the crowded environs of Tokyo just the day after the surrender ceremonies aboard the Missouri. I believe none of us had ever been in Japan before, so that first trip into Tokyo was a culmination of our fondest dreams of all those war-torn years.

Komori remained concerned about the security situation throughout his relatively short stay in Japan working for the occupation. One of his first tasks, carried out on that very first day, was to find a suitable location to establish CIC headquarters in Tokyo, and he set it up on the first floor of

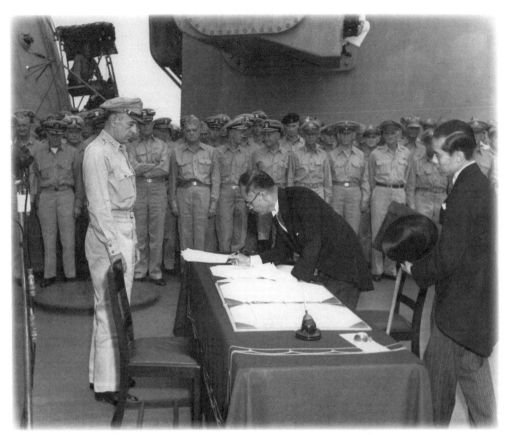

The war ended in the Pacific with the surrender of Japan to the Allied Powers aboard the USS Missouri on September 2, 1945. (Courtesy of the Naval History and Heritage Command)

the Daiichi Building. MacArthur's office had already been established on the fourth floor and Willoughby's on the second.

Once CIC moved into the building, Komori immediately moved to increase security, posting guards to prevent people from walking in without passes. However, there was only so much he could do about General MacArthur's lack of concern, and Komori wrote many years later that "he [MacArthur] was

INSTRUMENT OF SURRENDER

We, acting by command of and in behalf of the Emperor of Japan, the Japanese Government and the Japanese Imperial General Headquarters, hereby accept the provisions set forth in the declaration issued by the heads of the Governments of the United States, China and Great Britain on 26 July 1945, at Potsdam, and subsequently adhered to by the Union of Soviet Socialist Republics, which four powers are hereafter referred to as the Allied Powers.

We hereby proclaim the unconditional surrender to the Allied Powers of the Japanese Imperial General Headquarters and of all Japanese armed forces and all armed forces under Japanese control wherever situated.

We hereby command all Japanese forces wherever situated and the Japanese people to cease hostilities forthwith, to preserve and save from damage all ships, aircraft, and military and civil property and to comply with all requirements which may be imposed by the Supreme Commander for the Allied Powers or by agencies of the Japanese Government at his direction.

We hereby command the Japanese Imperial General Headquarters to issue at once orders to the Commanders of all Japanese forces and all forces under Japanese control wherever situated to surrender unconditionally themselves and all forces under their control.

We hereby command all civil, military and naval officials to obey and enforce all proclamations, orders and directives deemed by the Supreme Commander for the Allied Powers to be proper to effectuate this surrender and issued by him or under his authority and we direct all such officials to remain at their posts and to continue to perform their non-combatant duties unless specifically relieved by him or under his authority.

We hereby undertake for the Emperor, the Japanese Government and their successors to carry out the provisions of the Potsdam Declaration in good faith, and to issue whatever orders and take whatever action may be required by the Supreme Commander for the Allied Powers or by any other designated representative of the Allied Powers for the purpose of giving effect to that Declaration.

We hereby command the Japanese Imperial Government and the Japanese Imperial General Headquarters at once to liberate all allied prisoners of war and civilian internees now under Japanese control and to provide for their protection, care, maintenance and immediate transportation to places as directed.

The authority of the Emperor and the Japanese Government to rule the state shall be subject to the Supreme Commander for the Allied Powers who will take such steps as he deems proper to effectuate these terms of surrender.

Instrument of surrender signed at Tokyo Bay
(Each page of original document 15½ by 22¼ inches)

Page twelve

The Instrument of Surrender signed by the Japanese spelled out the terms of the surrender and post-war occupation. (Courtesy of the National Archives)

Signed at TOKYO BAY, JAPAN at 0904. I
on the _____ SECOND _____ day of ___ SEPTEMBER ___, 1945.

重光 葵

By Command and in behalf of the Emperor of Japan
and the Japanese Government.

梅津美治郎

By Command and in behalf of the Japanese
Imperial General Headquarters.

Accepted at TOKYO BAY, JAPAN at 0903 I
on the _____ SECOND _____ day of ___ SEPTEMBER ___, 1945,
for the United States, Republic of China, United Kingdom and the
Union of Soviet Socialist Republics, and in the interests of the other
United Nations at war with Japan.

Supreme Commander for the Allied Powers.

United States Representative

Republic of China Representative

United Kingdom Representative

Union of Soviet Socialist Republics
Representative

Commonwealth of Australia Representative

Dominion of Canada Representative

Provisional Government of the French
Republic Representative

Kingdom of the Netherlands Representative

Dominion of New Zealand Representative

Page thirteen

The Instrument of Surrender that ended the war was signed by representatives of all the Allied Powers. (Courtesy of the National Archives)

General Douglas MacArthur, Supreme Commander of the Allied Powers (SCAP), is seen leaving the Daiichi Building in Tokyo where SCAP headquarters was housed. (Courtesy of Sheldon Varney)

well known for his 'no body-guard' policy" and that he "did not mind children waving flags at the main entrance when it was time for his hopping into his Cadillac after work."

Komori remained in Japan from August 31 until November 3, 1945. While there, MacArthur presented Komori with a samurai sword forged on Sado-Shima by the sword-smith Fujiwara Motohiko in 1866. Documentation with the sword, including the kanji engraved into the sword itself, indicates that it was forged at the time of the Satsuma family's rebellion against the Tokugawa shogunate in support of the emperor and the imperial household. In return, Komori gifted MacArthur with the Burberry coat that became a part of his iconic post-war look. Komori brought the sword back to Hawai'i with him, and it is on display today at the Kaua'i Veterans Museum.

This high level of mutual respect was also evident in the work they did together to establish the occupation. As he had done early in the war, Komori helped set the tone for how the

This Tokugawa-era samurai sword, given to Komori by General Douglas MacArthur, is on display at the Kaua'i Veterans Museum. (Courtesy of Yoshinobu Oshiro)

US occupiers would treat the defeated Japanese. Moulin wrote in *American Samurais* that

> the Japanese were afraid and distrustful of the un-
> known alien conquerors, and dreaded any encounter
> with them. However, when they saw the MIS Nisei
> who spoke their language and dealt with them with
> understanding, their fears turned to relief. Eventu-
> ally, their suspicion turned to trust, and their initial
> antagonism turned to friendliness.

As the Supreme Commander of the Allied Powers for the occupation, MacArthur supported and modeled this tone, an attitude he described twenty years later when he noted that, "like the atom, language can be employed not only in waging war, but also in our quest for world peace."

Komori recorded his feelings about the historic events he was not just living through, but helping to shape, in a poem written as he left Japan to return to his own country, putting the war behind him.

Questions & Reflections of the War

Limitless waves, what can you tell of trends,
As I sit here seeking your intonations,
As to the true progress of foes and friends,
In course of world-wide brutish fight of nations?

Evergreen jungles, what is hidden there,
That we have left in your enfolding clutches,
Aside from hellish camps, fox-holes, and fear,
In days when men played hide and seek in searches?

Boundless terrain, what shells and arms lie spent,
Exhausted now with traces of some struggles,
That rose and fell in tides that came and went,
From precipice to shores where fly the gulls?

The waters answer but a swishing sound,
As if too pained to tell of muddied battles.
The leaves flutter a sigh as if to drown,
The foreign sounds of dropping blood and metals.
The ground but quakes in tremors, nights and days,
From night more fits of crawling boots and bodies,
While Heaven shines always with sparkling rays,
And nebulae rush round in whirlpool eddies.

11 November 1945
Tokyo

CHAPTER 4

Enemies both Foreign
and Domestic

Following the war, Komori returned to the Japanese community of post-war Hawai'i.
(Courtesy of Hawai'i State Archives)

A lthough World War II was now officially over, another
threat to US security crept up during the three months
that Arthur Komori worked for the occupation in Japan:
the Communist threat. While the United States and other
Western nations had been concerned with the threat of
Communism ever since the early twentieth century, it lost

much of its negative association for a short time during the war while the United States and the Soviet Union fought as allies. But the uneasy truce came to an end with the end of the war, and the anti-communist sentiment that would reach a peak in the 1950s with the Red Scare led by Senator Joseph McCarthy and the House Committee on Un-American Activities began anew.

In Japan, the Communist Party had been founded in 1922 and was almost immediately outlawed with the passage of the Peace Preservation Law in 1925. In 1928, under this law, the government arrested over 1,600 Communist Party members, most of whom remained incarcerated when the war ended in 1945. One of MacArthur's primary goals as the Supreme Commander for the Allied Powers (SCAP) was to democratize Japan, and while relations between the United States and the Soviet Union deteriorated quickly following the war, resulting in a "red purge" in occupied Japan in 1950, General MacArthur began the occupation in 1945 by issuing a series of civil rights orders that included the release of all Communist prisoners.

Komori later described his dealings with the Japanese communists, for whom he seemed to hold some respect, despite having little sympathy for their views.

When the Japanese Communist leaders were liberated from prison, Agent Masuda and I interviewed them

Japanese Communist Party Secretary General Kyuichi Tokuda, shown here, was released from prison, along with other imprisoned Communist Party members, in one of General MacArthur's first acts as the Supreme Commander for the Allied Powers. (Courtesy of Getty Images)

at a special reception for them at GHQ, Daiichi Building. . . . Though ravenously hungry, and unaccustomed to haranguing at length after their long confinement, to see the gradual flaming of their smoldering sparks of Communistic ideals was an education for all. I believed Secretary-General [of the Japanese Communist Party] Tokuda when he told me that they would have easily died had they not kept a steadfast resolve in their hearts for their ideals.

They were, he noted, "so fanatical that they were trying to convince us of Communism by the time they had finished eating." But he also commented that, "it embarrassed me to no end to see Tokuda come stealing up to my desk in the 441st thereafter and greeting me like a long-lost comrade. When more guards were installed at all entrances into GHQ, it put a stop to unexpected guests."

Arthur Komori returned to Hawai'i in November and was eventually joined by his wife Marie and daughter Rosemary, who arrived in April 1946 on the SS *Lurline*, part of a "load of war brides." On December 8, 1945, Komori reenlisted as a Master Sergeant in the 401st CIC Detachment in Honolulu in "a strictly under-cover capacity requiring the wearing of civilian clothes." Once again Komori found himself going undercover in the Japanese community, as he had done in Manila, but this time it was the Japanese American community of Hawai'i where he had grown up. From this position as a member of the community, he "engaged in various investigations of subversive organizations and individuals in Hawaii."

Komori's work during this post-war period in Honolulu mirrored much of what he had done at the end of the war in Manila and in Tokyo as the occupation was beginning—the basic work of a CIC agent. In this capacity as an agent of military security, he conducted security surveys of military installations as well as interviews of references, leads, contacts, and informants in loyalty investigations. He also tested applicants for Civil Service translator and interpreter duties in Japan and "maintained liaison with the FBI, ONI

[Office of Naval Intelligence], and police agencies to fulfill the mission of CIC in the Pacific theatre." But there was also the added element of his investigations of the domestic situation, which Komori later described as "investigating the communist leaders preaching strikes, Japanese leaders inciting pro-Japan propaganda." The members of the Subversive Section of the CIC, he wrote, specialized in continual research and investigations on "communist party members, suspects, and sympathizers" and were, he noted, "given intensive orientation, guidance, and training in the field of communism by [Special Agent William] Bill Doyle and [FBI Communist Section Chief] Major Sweeny."

The nature of this work was secretive, and we are left with few details about what he did, but even this is addressed in unpublished memoirs when he wrote that, "disinformation was part of our undercover strategy." However, we do see evidence of the high regard in which Komori was held by his superior officers in the freedom he had at this time to do whatever he saw fit in this large interlocking area. He was given free access to the civilian community by the FBI and communicated pertinent information to Special Agent William Doyle, FBI Communist Section Chief through "weekly consolidated reports on Communism, labor trends, subversive activities, and general trends in the Japanese community of interest to the Commanding General, FBI, ONI, and Chief, CIC."

These brief descriptions in Komori's later writings make reference to many aspects of the complex picture that emerged in the post-war years in Hawai'i, which he and his fellow Subversive Section officers would be responsible for fleshing out for both the local and national law enforcement communities. One of these was the conflation of labor unions, and in particular the International Longshore and Warehouse Union (ILWU), with communism. Another was the tendency for the returning Nisei veterans to align themselves with the emerging Democratic Party, which itself was allied with the labor movement. Nisei soldiers were returning from the war having fought and died, as Komori later put it, "to prove our loyalty and to prove that our parents were also loyal to the American cause," and they were not willing to settle for second-class citizenship. No more would their existence be dictated by the bosses on the plantations. It was in this context that many Nisei became involved with the Democratic Party and, by extension, the unions. But given their strong sense of patriotism and their recent record of valor in the war, it is not at all clear that this new political activism could be equated with a sympathy for, much less direct involvement with, communism. Yet there is evidence that the labor movement was perceived as being associated with communism in the minds of the people of Hawai'i. In the Ignacio revolt in December 1947, for example, Amos Ignacio, vice-president of the Hawai'i Island division of the United Sugar Workers,

ILWU Local 142, broke away to form the short-lived Union of Hawaiian Workers because, as he said, he wanted to be a free man and wanted no part of communism.

But despite this complicated local situation, on the national scene, this association between labor rights and communism was strong, and Komori worked, not for a local entity, but for the US Army and federal civilian law enforcement agencies. So it is not surprising that his work reflected the strong anti-communist feelings that were prevalent in the government at the start of the Cold War. The US Department of Justice had begun keeping a list of organizations it deemed subversive in 1942, and by March 1947, elaborate loyalty requirements had been established for all federal employees. We know from his writings that Komori's work included conducting these loyalty investigations. We also know that when Hawai'i Governor Ingram Stainback tied Hawai'i's emerging labor movement to communism in a speech he gave on Armistice Day in 1947 at the National Memorial Cemetery of the Pacific at Punchbowl, his statements were based on information provided by military intelligence sources, that is, intelligence Komori and his fellow CIC officers were gathering in the Nisei community in Honolulu.

With the very little firsthand information we have about this period of his career, it is hard for us to know how Komori felt about the situation in Hawai'i. On the one hand, we know that he was a loyal and patriotic member of the CIC

Jiro Yukimura, who also served in the MIS, was a fellow Kaua'i resident and acquaintance of Komori's since before the war. (Courtesy of the Honolulu Star-Advertiser)

throughout his career, and that the threat of communism was taken very seriously in the nation at the time. But on the other hand, many of the members of the Japanese community in Hawai'i were people he had known for years—often fellow veterans—and he had no doubt of their patriotism. One example of this dichotomy is the story of Jiro Yukimura, a fellow MIS veteran who had returned to his home on Kaua'i following the war. Yukimura, who had completed his college degree before the war, nevertheless had the benefits of the GI Bill available to him when he returned, and he decided to take a night course in Russian. This immediately put him under suspicion, and it was not known whether or not Komori had been involved in investigating him. However, in being interviewed for this book, Yukimura said that Komori would never have questioned his motives, the two had known each other since before the war, and Komori would know that there was nothing suspicious in his behavior. He felt certain it was someone from the mainland who had raised the questions.

Komori remained in his position in the 401ˢᵗ Detachment, CIC, in Honolulu until November 1949. But he did have one assignment that took him out of his undercover role, back into uniform, and back into the Western Pacific. From January 9 to May 6, 1948, Komori served as part of Joint Task Force Seven as a security agent for the second atomic test held at Eniwetok Atoll in the Marshall Islands. In his various memoirs, Komori mentioned this assignment only in passing. Yet, in hindsight, this was one more historic event at which he was present and another incident in which he demonstrated his bravery and loyalty to his country.

In a series of notes on his military career written in 1989, he referred to his assignment to Joint Task Force Seven as a "MISSION UNIQUE," a phrase he emphasized by writing it in all capital letters, but which he then said nothing more about. He also described it briefly in an interview he gave to the Kauaʻi Museum in 1992: "Eniwetok was an atoll, like all the other atolls, surrounded by reefs and islands. We had to patrol all those islands to make sure there weren't any spies from Russia, for example, spying on the test." He went on to say that "when the bomb exploded, we were all in garb, you know, protection from radioactive rays," even though they were twenty-five miles from the explosion. "To witness one of those things. . ." he added, trailing off. Clearly in hindsight, he was still amazed by what he had seen that day. But on that day, he was, as one would expect, all business. He described how the samples that were to be delivered to Washington were collected:

> After the bombs exploded, specimens were gathered by planes flying through the clouds. And we would carry the specimens as couriers to Washington DC Three of us were couriers, from the atolls to Hickam to Edwards, and finally to Andrews.

A restricted memo from Headquarters Joint Task Force Seven names Komori and his two fellow officers and gives some sense of the importance of the mission:

> Travel by military, naval, or commercial aircraft from Eniwetok to destination is directed except where other means of authorized travel are equally or more expeditious and is necessary for the successful completion of an urgent mission directly related to the emergency,

The United States carried out nuclear tests on Eniwetok from 1948 until 1958. (Courtesy of the Defense Nuclear Agency)

and "Commanding Officers of all posts, camps, and stations are requested to furnish such motor transportation as may be necessary for the successful completion of this mission."

Whether or not the three-person security team required extraordinary cooperation from the commanding officers of the "posts, camps, or stations" between Eniwetok Atoll and Washington, DC, the mission was completed successfully with their arrival at the Washington headquarters of Joint Task Force Seven in April 1948. While in Washington, Komori took the opportunity to visit his wartime commanding officer Major General Thorpe (his "first and only Chief of Counterintelligence from 1942 to 1945") who was working in the Pentagon. Komori told Thorpe that he had just taken the test for CIC Warrant Officer, and Thorpe sent him to "see his friend in charge." Komori was commissioned a Regular Army Warrant Officer, Counterintelligence, in December of that year.

Komori returned to Honolulu following his special assignment to Joint Task Force Seven and spent another year in the 401st CIC Detachment in Honolulu. In November 1949, he moved with his wife Marie and daughter Rosemary to Maryland, where he joined the faculty of the CIC School at Fort Holabird in Baltimore.

Komori taught at the CIC School at Fort Holabird in Baltimore, Maryland from 1949 to 1956.

While still in the army, Komori finally found himself living a normal, domestic lifestyle. Rosemary later wrote about this period, recalling playing catch in the backyard with her Dad, going ice-skating together, and getting her first swimming lesson from her Dad in the Chesapeake Bay.

Komori was commissioned a First Lieutenant when he joined the CIC School faculty, where his initial appointment was as a Japanese-language instructor. A year later, in November 1950, he joined the school's department of international affairs. In this new role, by his own description, he "conducted classes in the whole field of subjects pertaining to the Far East, specializing in Japan, China, Korea, Southeast Asia, and the Philippines." He also wrote that he "maintained large files and compiled up-to-date lectures by constant research in classified intelligence documents in the Secret Files of the CIC School Library." Even in the role of professor, it seems Komori had a hard time giving up his intelligence role and went above and beyond to make sure that a new generation of CIC officers went into the field well prepared. In his memoirs he wrote that he

> would teach them what the agents would do under certain circumstances in Korea and Japan. The Korean War had just started, too, so they were sending quite a few of the agents out to Korea. We had interrogations, and lessons in arrests of persons. . . .

Komori remained at the school for the rest of his regular army career, as well as for an additional four years as a civilian instructor. Komori's army career ended in 1952 when he resigned his commission in protest over President Harry Truman's firing of General MacArthur, the latest example of the personal loyalty to MacArthur he had developed early in the war in Bataan and Corregidor. Upon leaving the army in 1952, he transferred to the Air Force Reserve at the rank of Captain. He also took advantage of his GI Bill benefit to attend law school at the University of Maryland with, as he noted, the blessing of his superiors. We also see, in his memoirs, how settled his home life was during this period, despite his continued involvement in training agents for a counterintelligence role during war. Komori described his life at the time as "like a university professor two hours a day, and the rest of the day to do my thing, which was study law."

Arthur Komori graduated from the University of Maryland law school in 1954. He returned to Hawai'i with his family in 1956 and pursued a career as a lawyer. The family spent a few years in Honolulu, during which Komori served for a short time as Deputy Attorney General of the state of Hawai'i. He eventually settled on Kaua'i where he served as president of the Kaua'i MIS veterans club from 1959 to 1962. He continued to practice law and served as a magistrate in the district of Waimea. Komori remained on Kaua'i until his death in 2000.

CHAPTER 5

A Lifetime of Loyalty

The service of MIS WWII veterans was finally recognized in 2000. (Courtesy of the William J. Clinton Presidential Library)

The army career of Arthur Komori was unique in so many ways. Yet his story nevertheless epitomizes, in many ways, the experience of the American Nisei of his generation. The unique timing of their situation—the first generation of their family born in the US and coming of age just as Japan entered into war against the United States—meant that demonstrating their patriotism necessarily involved overtly rejecting the country and culture of their ancestors. Seemingly to a man, they decided on loyalty to the land of their birth, and in Komori's case, personal loyalty to the man who had shown so much trust in him, General Douglas MacArthur.

In his book *Nisei Linguists*, McNaughton noted that, "no amount of Nisei cooperation or fervent declarations of patriotism . . . could allay white suspicions that at least some Nisei might prove disloyal." He added that, "the Nisei would have to demonstrate their loyalty in action under the most difficult circumstances, but first they would have to be given the chance to do so." Komori had been very much aware of this when he wrote about his initial recruitment that "it was a heaven-sent opportunity to prove ourselves" and that "we felt keenly our responsibility for the sake of our fellow Japanese-Americans . . . and for the sake of our alien parents." There is ample evidence that, by the end of the war, the men in charge of prosecuting the war—those who had worked closely with the Nisei and saw the impact of their work—valued the Nisei and their service very highly. President Roosevelt, himself, expressed this sentiment on the occasion of the activation of the 442nd Regimental Combat Team. His comments that day showed a clear departure from his earlier actions in signing Executive Order 9066, which authorized the internment of Americans of Japanese ancestry:

No loyal citizen of the United States should be denied the democratic right to exercise the responsibilities of his citizenship, regardless of his ancestry. The principle on which this country was founded and by which it has always been governed is that Americanism is a matter of the mind and heart; Americanism is not, and never was, a matter of race or ancestry.

Japanese Americans in Southern California wait to board a train that will take them to an internment camp. (Courtesy of the National Archives)

General MacArthur testified to the fact that there was not a single instance of sabotage or treason by Japanese Americans. Major General Willoughby, MacArthur's Chief of Intelligence, was eager to make known his feelings about the war-time work of Japanese Americans in a speech to the House of Representatives in 1967: Having "long sought an opportunity to record the remarkable contributions of the Nisei in war and peace, and perhaps atone for barbaric injustices inflicted upon them," he noted that the Nisei had served with "spectacular brilliance unsurpassed by any comparable American or Allied military unit." Colonel Mashbir, Commandant of ATIS, noted in his book, *I Was an American Spy*, that, "the United States of America owes a debt to these men and to their families which it can never fully repay."

And yet, as we have seen in Komori's story, the challenges these men faced in carrying out this work were many. Some of these challenges—those related either to their race or to the secret nature of their work—Komori shared with his fellow Nisei in the MIS.

Others were not shared with either his fellow Nisei soldiers or his non-Japanese fellow CIC agents, but resulted from the unique combination of his being both a Nisei and a CIC agent. There are many examples of occasions when he placed himself in great danger while accepting the fact that he was outside the army bureaucracy and could not count on

GENERAL HEADQUARTERS
UNITED STATES ARMY FORCES, PACIFIC
Office of the Chief of Counter Intelligence

Advance Echelon
APO 500
3 November 1945

SUBJECT: Commendation

TO   : Master Sergeant ARTHUR S. KOMORI 10100023

     I desire to commend you for the excellent work you have done as a member of the Counter-Intelligence Section in this theater throughout the war. Your efforts have been continuous from Bataan to Japan during which time your devotion and loyalty to your country has been an example for other men to emulate. The value of your contribution to the intelligence service of the Army was large.

E. R. THORPE
Brigadier General, U. S. Army
Chief of Counter Intelligence

Although official recognitions were scarce, it is clear from memos such as this one written by Brigadier General Elliott Thorpe that Komori's commanding officers recognized and valued his work.

its protection. He described many occasions when he worked not only without recognition of his contributions, but often with suspicion and derision from his fellow Americans. Yet, he continued to display his strong sense of responsibility and patriotism throughout the war and into his post-war career. In all the records Komori left of his military career, the overwhelming theme is one of patriotism and duty. A 1945 memo addressed simply "To the Officer in Charge," wherein he described the many occasions when he had met with a lack of respect in the course of his work, represents a rare record of dissatisfaction. For the most part, Komori's feelings upon his original enlistment in 1941, "that we had been chosen for our loyalty, and we felt honored," and that "above all, we wanted to prove worthy of the high trust placed in us," were still strong when he returned home from the war in 1945.

Belated Recognition

Those who worked with Komori clearly valued his service and considered him a tremendous asset. The secretive nature of his job, however, meant that, even within the army, his story was not well known. Although Komori's commanding officers recommended him for the Purple Heart, the Silver Star, and Bronze Star, with the earliest recommendation coming as early as June 1942, Komori received only a single award during his military career. The Bronze Star was awarded for his service in Manila in December 1945, with the war over and Komori back in Honolulu. Komori understood the challenges inherent in decorating an intelligence man, and was grateful to Generals Willoughby and Thorpe, who "dared to decorate my valor."

Recognition for members of the Military Intelligence Service was no more forthcoming following the war than it had been during the war. While members of the 442nd Regimental Combat Team and the 100th Battalion were recognized soon after the end of the war, documents relating to the MIS remained classified until the 1970s. President Nixon signed Executive Order 11652 in 1972, which set up a schedule of declassification for these documents. Then, in 1974, a set of Privacy Act Amendments to the Freedom of Information Act of 1966 were enacted in a congressional override of President Ford's veto. Before these acts, the secrecy had been so absolute that veterans of the MIS had not even told their families about their experiences during the war. Rosemary Anzai, Arthur Komori's daughter, described her father's experience with this secrecy, writing in his voice in an account of her parent's life taken from, among other sources, his letters to her:

> We who survived the war have innumerable stories that have been kept from the public eye. My fellow MIS officers and I had been sworn to secrecy about our clandestine activities until this ban was lifted in 1974. Only then could our families begin to comprehend what we had gone through in service to our country. MIS veterans had been required to share

this code of silence, which took its toll on many a family. When we could finally speak freely, it was tough to open up and share our wartime experiences. I found that I could not talk openly with my wife and daughter about the ordeals I had gone through. How could they fathom the darkness of it all? Death, carnage, mayhem, pretense and intrigue; footsteps in dark alleys; eating monkey meat to avoid malaria in the jungle. Many veterans remained silent—never able to erase the hellish memories of the war. Nightmares haunted me the rest of my life.

In 1988, Arthur Komori was among the first class of inductees into the Military Intelligence Corp Hall of Fame at Fort Huachuca, Arizona. The letter from Major General Julius Parker, then Chief of Military Intelligence, congratulating him on his selection acknowledged "the many contributions you made to the Corps during your illustrious career." No further recognition came during his lifetime.

Arthur Komori passed away February 17, 2000, less than two months before he and his unit were awarded the Presidential Unit Citation with two Oak Leaf Clusters by President Bill Clinton on April 3, an award that had been received by the 442nd Regimental Combat Team and the 100th Battalion in August 1945, fifty-five years earlier. In awarding the citation, President Clinton noted their "extraordinary heroism in military operations" during the Battle of

MIS veterans were awarded the Presidential Unit Citation with two Oak Leaf Clusters by President Bill Clinton in a ceremony held on April 3, 2000. (Courtesy of the William J. Clinton Presidential Library)

Corregidor, and also acknowledged that "rarely has a nation been so well-served by a people who it ill-treated." Further recognition followed in 2011 when members of the MIS, 100th Battalion, and 442nd Regimental Combat Team were awarded the Congressional Gold Medal, America's highest civilian award, on November 2, 2011. All members of these units, whether living or dead, received this recognition in a special ceremony in Washington, DC.

This Congressional Gold Medal was created for the members of the MIS, 100th Battalion, and 442nd Regimental Combat Team in 2011. (Courtesy of the US Army Institute of Heraldry)

President Obama signed the bill that awarded the Congressional Gold Medal to members of the MIS, 100th Battalion, and 442nd Regimental Combat Team in October 2010. (Courtesy of the White House, photo by Pete Souza)

Duty, honor, country

Duty, honor, country, those three hallowed words reverently dictate what you ought to be, what you can be, what you will be.

These words from General MacArthur's farewell address to the Corps of Cadets during his final visit to West Point are a fitting epigraph to the story of Arthur Komori's life and military career. Throughout his life, Komori harbored a strong personal loyalty to MacArthur, noting as late as 1989 his belief in MacArthur's "god-like power over all he came across." He also maintained a deep pride in the actions of his fellow Nisei during the war. To him, one of their greatest accomplishments was unlocking a window of opportunity for individuals of Japanese ancestry nation-wide. Komori had absolute faith that the loyalty he and his fellow Nisei in the MIS demonstrated to the nation helped persuade the army to send the 442nd Infantry Regiment and 100th Infantry Battalion into battle, and further, that the heroism and exemplary record of these men, more visible than that of their MIS counterparts, did much to sway the anti-Japanese American sentiment. He talked about this in a 1979 interview with *The Honolulu Advertiser,* saying that, "the work he and his associates did. . . changed the status of Americans of Japanese ancestry in the United States." "I think it was because of our record that we have Niseis in all fields of endeavor," he added. Although Komori was willing to die for his country, in the end it was his life and the lives of his fellow servicemen that created a better future for generations of Japanese Americans to come.

And in keeping with his personality and his record of exemplary service, Komori's dedication to his country's cause remained resolute through his life. He wrote in 1969, in a piece he titled "Vivid Recollections," about the contributions of, as well as the debt owed to, all veterans:

> Americans back home. . . must never forget the veterans of such wars and their rehabilitation. All our sufferings and tortures, of the Bataan Death March and present-day Communist mistreatment of prisoners in Vietnam and Korea can never be atoned for, nor forgotten. . . . I look back over my career and try to assess whether in a small measure I could say that my life and activities have not been spent in vain, and that I had contributed as a member of my race, and as a member of a larger society, to make this world a better place to live in. . . . In the final analysis it was something worth fighting for, to preserve and to foster. And to those of us who died, and partially died out there, I say, we have not lost whatever we left behind in vain.

BIBLIOGRAPHY

Anzai, Rosemary. *For Love of Country: WWII Secret Agent Arthur Komori.* Orange, CA: The Paragon Agency, 2013.

Bray, Ann. "Undercover Nisei." In *Military Intelligence: Its Heroes and Legends*, compiled by Diane L. Hamm, 29–45. Honolulu, HI: University Press of the Pacific, 2001.

Curtis, Paul. "MIS saved lives in WWII." *Garden Island* (Līhuʻe, HI), November 12, 1999.

———. "VA makes exception, OKs benefits for Komori." *Garden Island* (Kauaʻi, HI), November 20, 1999.

———. "Kauaians in military intelligence in WWII finally get unit citation." *Garden Island* (Kauaʻi, HI), July 3, 2000.

Daws, Gavan. *Shoal of Time.* Honolulu, HI: University of Hawaiʻi Press, 1989.

Edwards, Duvall. *Spy Catchers of the US Army in the War with Japan: The Unfinished Story of the Counter Intelligence Corps.* Gig Harbor, WA: Red Apple Publishing, 1994.

Gordon, John. *Fighting for MacArthur, The Navy and Marine Corps' Desperate Defense of the Philippines.* Annapolis, MD: Naval Institute Press, 2011.

Harrington, Joseph D. *Yankee Samurai: The Secret Role of Nisei in America's Pacific Victory.* Detroit, MI: Pettigrew Enterprises, Inc., 1979.

Hawaii Nikkei History Editorial Board. *Japanese Eyes, American Heart: Voices from the Home Front in World War II Hawaii.* Edited by Gail Miyasaki. Vol. 2. Honolulu, HI: Tendai Educational Foundation, 1998.

Holmes, T. Michael. *The Specter of Communism in Hawaii.* Honolulu, HI: University of Hawaiʻi Press, 1994.

Horne, Gerald. *Fighting in Paradise: Labor Unions, Racism, and Communists in the Making of Modern Hawai'i.* Honolulu, HI: University of Hawai'i Press, 2011.

Ichinokuchi, Tad. *John Aiso and the MIS: Japanese-American Soldiers in the Military Intelligence Service, World War II.* Los Angeles, CA: Military Intelligence Service Club of Southern California, 1988.

Mashbir, Sidney. *I was an American Spy.* Manhattan, NY: Vantage Press, 1953.

McNaughton, James. *Nisei Linguists: Japanese Americans in the Military Intelligence Service during World War II.* Washington, DC: Department of the Army, 2006.

———. "Nisei Linguists and New Perspectives on the Pacific War: Intelligence, Race, and Continuity." In *The U.S. Army and World War II: Selected Papers from the Army's Commemorative Conferences,* edited by Judith L. Bellafaire, Fort McNair, DC: Center of Military History, United States Army, 1998, 371–381.

Military Intelligence Service Veterans Club of Hawaii. *Secret Valor: M.I.S. Personnel, World War II, Pacific Theater, Pre Pearl Harbor to Sept. 8, 1951.* Honolulu, HI: Military Intelligence Service Veterans Club of Hawaii, 1993.

Moulin, Pierre. *American Samurais: WWII in the Pacific.* Alexandria, VA: Socrates Institute Press, 2011.

Murphy, Thomas D. *Ambassadors in Arms.* Honolulu, HI: University of Hawai'i Press, 1954.

Nakatsuka, Lawrence. "Only Hawaii Survivor of Bataan Tells Story of 11th Hour Escape." *Honolulu Star-Bulletin,* April 17–8, 1944.

Sakakida, Richard and Wayne S. Kiyosaki. *A Spy in Their Midst: The World War II Struggle of a Japanese-American Hero.* Lanham, MD: Madison Books, 1995.

Sayer, Ian and Douglas Botting. *America's Secret Army: The Untold Story of the Counter Intelligence Corps.* In US Congress. Congressional Record. 104th Cong., 2d sess., 1996, Vol. 142, pt. 2, at 1616-1621. http://www.fas.org/irp/congress/1996_cr/s960130a.htm.

Shirley, Orville C. *Americans: The Story of the 442nd Combat Team.* Washington, DC: Infantry Journal Press, 1946. http://www.internmentarchives.com/showdoc.php?docid=00010&search_id=45150&pagenum=1.

TenBruggencate, Jan. "Manila, 1941: Toasting Japan for Uncle Sam." *Honolulu Advertiser,* June 12, 1979.

United States Army Military History Institute. *Counter Intelligence Corps History and Mission in World War II.* Baltimore, MD: Army Counter Intelligence Corps School, 1951.

Uyeda, Clifford and Barry Saiki, eds. *The Pacific War and Peace, Americans of Japanese Ancestry in Military Intelligence Service 1941 to 1952.* San Francisco, CA: Military Intelligence Service Association of Northern California and the National Japanese American Historical Society, 1991.

Wakukawa, Ernest K. *A History of the Japanese People in Hawaii.* Honolulu, HI: The Toyo Shin, 1938.

Zalburg, Sanford. *A Spark is Struck: Jack Hall and the ILWU in Hawaii.* Honolulu, HI: Watermark Publishing, 2007.

INDEX

Aborigines, Australian, training of, 65

Allied Translator and Interpreter Section (ATIS): creation of, 60–61; importance of, 63–64; secrecy, 64

alternating three-day shifts on Bataan and Corregidor, 43

American Legion, 4

anti-Japanese sentiment: by Komori, 5; among American troops, 20; in the US, 8

Anzai, Rosemary (daughter): arrival in Hawai'i, 94; born, 81; on secrecy, 111–112

Army Air Force Cadet Flight Training, Komori's rejection from, 6

atomic tests at Eniwetok Atoll, 99–101

Australian Outback, Komori's description of, 65–66

Bamboo Headquarters: description of, 36; establishment of, 34

Bataan: alternating shifts, 43; Death March, 47, 116; falls to Japan, 46; Komori's description of the battle of

in *Honolulu Star Bulletin*, 69; US evacuation to, 29

Bilibid Prison, Old, Komori incarcerated in, 24–25

born, 3

Boy Scouts, 4, 5

Bradford, Bill, 47–48

Bronze Star awarded, 110

Camp Savage, Minnesota, Komori as student and teacher, 66–68

Central Intermediate School: attendance at, 3; site of recruitment interview, 9

Chiang Kai-shek: evacuation of emissary, 47; Pacific forces, 8

Christmas dinner 1941, 33

Church of the Crossroads, 4

citizenship, dual, xiii–xiv

Civil Aviation Academy (CAA) flight school, 4

Clinton, President Bill, 112–113

Cold War, 97

Communism: in Japan, 92–93; in post-war US, 91–97; Secretary General Kyuichi Tokuda, 93–94 confidence of US troops, 43–44

Congressional Gold Medal, 113–114

Congressional Record, account of warfare in Bataan in, 36

Corps of Intelligence Police (CIP): Komori and Sakakida recruited to, 11; mission, 15; name changed to CIC, 33; part of US Army's G2 (Intelligence) Division, 13

Corregidor: alternating shifts, 43; evacuation to, 29; Japanese attack on, 33; last Allied holdout, 47

Counter Intelligence Corps (CIC): formerly Corps of Intelligence Police, 33; headquarters in Bataan, 41; headquarters in Tokyo 82–83; Komori as advocate for, 56, 58; Komori and Sakakida as first CIC agents attached to combat troops in battle, 34; lack of recognition of, 56, 58, 74; role in Australia, 60; role in liberated Manila, 74; search for agents left behind, 72

Counter Intelligence Corp (CIC) School: at Brisbane, 66; at Fort Holabird, Baltimore, 102; faculty at, 103; civilian faculty at, 104

cover story, 17–18

danger: of being shot by US troops, 37; of treatment if captured by Japanese, 46

Democratic Party, 96

Department of Information, Melbourne, 69

diaries of Japanese soldiers, 41

died, 112

Doyle, William, 95

Drisko, Grenfell, 19, 25

empire building by Japan, 8

enemy identification service, in Bataan, 38

Eniwetok Atoll, Marshall Islands, 99–101

enlistment, 12

Europe first strategy, 29, 44

evacuation: of Komori from the Philippines, 46–51; of MacArthur from the Philippines, 46; of Manila, 29–33

Evans, Colonel, memo of commendation from, 55

Executive Order 9066, 106

Field Security Section School, Brisbane, 66

Ford, President Gerald, 111

Fort Santiago, 20, 25

Fort Holabird, 102

442nd Regimental Combat Team, formation of, 106

friendly fire, 37–38

G2: evacuation from Corregidor to Bataan, 33; evacuation from Manila, 29–33

Gilbert, Major Jack, 9, 11

Gunn, Paul "Pappy," 50–51

Hachiya, Frank, 37–38

Hawai'i National Guard, Komori's rejection from, 6

International Longshore and Warehouse Union (ILWU), 96–97

internment camps, 62

interpreter: Komori's role at the Japanese surrender ceremony, 79; during entry into Japan, 82

interrogation of Japanese prisoners: first, 27; in Bataan, 38; in liberated Manila, 75; techniques, 28, 75; treating them kindly, 27, 28, 74, 75; definitive report on, 28–29, 58

interviews of Komori: by *Honolulu Advertiser*, 36; by *Honolulu Star Bulletin*, 37, 48, 68–69; by Kaua'i Museum, 64–65, 100

isolation: Komori's feelings of, 26, 108–110; relief from in ATIS, 62

Japanese Americans: internment of, 62, 77, 106; impact of Nisei's war service's on, 106, 115–116; Komori's impact on, 11–12

Japanese language classes, 3

Japanese in the Philippines, history of, 15–16

jungle warfare, 36

Kempeitai (Japanese military police), 34

Komori, Esther Kyoko (mother), 3

Komori, Rosemary (daughter). *See* Anzai, Rosemary

Komori, Yoshitaro (father), 3

K-T Flight School, 4, 50

labor unions, 96–97

language, as secret weapon, 63, 64

law school, University of Maryland, 104

linguists, Nisei: arrival at ATIS, 61; impact on Japanese Americans, 106, 115–116; Komori's pride in, 62; secrecy of role, 63 loyalty: of Komori to America, 5, 11, 38, 106; of Nisei, 63, 106; Sakakida's, 77. *See also* patriotism

loyalty investigations: in Australia, 60; in post-war Hawai'i, 97

MacArthur, General Douglas: accepted Japanese surrender, 81; declared Manila an open city, 33; evacuation to Australia, 46; farewell address to West Point Corps of Cadets, 115; firing of, 104; Komori's loyalty to, 40, 104, 106, 115; ordered to evacuate from the Philippines, 29; revered by Komori, 38–39, 87–88, 115; statement about Nisei loyalty, 108; Supreme Commander of the Allied Powers, 81, 88, 92

malaria, 36

Malinta Tunnel: translation unit set up in, 41–43; working conditions in, 42–43

malnutrition, 36, 46

Manila: attacked by Japanese, 23; declared an open city, 33; Komori's arrival in, 14–15; Komori's employment in, 18; Komori's return to, 72; Komori's

working conditions in, 20; lodgings in, 17; overtaken by Japanese, 29; spies infiltrating, 75

Mashbir, Lieutenant Colonel Sidney: Commandant of ATIS, 61; on loyalty of Nisei, 63

Masuda, Hisashi "Johnny," 74, 75

Matsuoka, Yosuke, Japanese Foreign Minister, xiv

McKinley High School: attendance, 3; clubs, 4; graduation from, 4

Military Intelligence Corp Hall of Fame, Komori inducted into, 112

Military Intelligence Service (MIS): belated recognition for, 111–112; secrecy of work, 111

Military Intelligence Service Language School (MISLS), 60–61, 67

Missing in action, declaration of, 54

monkey, eating, 36

Nisei: contributions of, 108–109; loyalty of, 63, 106–108; post-war attitudes, 96; role in shortening war, 63

Nixon, President Richard, 111

Nu'uanu YMCA, 4

Obama, President Barack, 114

open city, 33

patriotism, 18, 110. *See also* loyalty

Pearl Harbor, bombing of, 23

poems by Komori: All, 43–44; The Austral Prayer, 52; Golden Hearts of Men of Steel, 40–41; Questions & Reflections of the War, 89; Victory March, 79–81

Poon, Marie N.: arrival in Hawai'i, 94; courtship of, 71–72

Pratt, C. Dudley, 5

Presidential Unit Citation with two Oak Leaf Clusters, 112

Privacy Act Amendments to the Freedom of Information Act of 1966, 111

Purple Heart, recommendation for, 54, 110

radiogram authorizing Komori's enlistment, 9,

Rank: immediate promotion upon swearing in, 12; "problem of" within CIC, 56–57

Raymond, Captain Nelson: as mentor, 20–21, 25, 38; contact with, 19; credit for security service in Bataan, 38; death, 47; faith in Nisei, 38; first meeting with Komori and Sakakida, 14–15, 16–17; recruited Yamagata, 34; role in Komori's evacuation from Bataan, 46

recommendations: for Bronze Star, 110; for Purple Heart, 54; for Silver Star, 55; from General Willoughby, 54–55; memo of commendation from Colonel Evans, 55,

recruitment, Komori's, 9–11

resignation in protest of MacArthur's firing, 104

Roosevelt, President Franklin Delano: on formation of the 442nd Regimental Combat Team, 106–107; ordered evacuation of the Philippines, 29

rumors about Komori's disappearance from Honolulu, 13–14, 69

Sakakida, Richard: decision not to evacuate, 47; recruitment procedure, 9–11; role during Japanese occupation of Manila, 26–27; supporting testimony from Komori, 75, 77 samurai sword given to Komori by MacArthur, 86–87

secrecy: of CIC work, 56, 69, 72–74; end of, 111; from families, 111; surrounding Komori's escape from Corregidor, 53; surrounding Komori's recruitment, 13–14; surrounding post-war work in Hawai'i, 95; of role of linguists in the Pacific war, 63

security: of front lines, 34; investigations, 60; post-war threat to, 91

Sharpe, General William F., 51

Silver Star, recommendation for, 55, 110

spies, infiltrating Manila, 75

subversive organizations and individuals, investigations of by Komori in post-war Hawai'i, 94–97

surrender, Japanese, 78, 81–82

swearing in, 12

Thorpe, Brigadier General Elliott: commendation by, 109; denial of permission to marry, 71; Komori as translator for, 82; reprimand from, 56; visit to in Washington D.C., 101–102

Tokuda, Kyuichi, Secretary General of the Japanese Communist Party, 93–94

Tokyo, Komori's arrival at, 81–82

training, formal: at Camp Savage, Minnesota, 66–67; at CIC School, Brisbane, 66; at Field Security Section School, Brisbane, 66; Komori's dual role in, 66–67

Tripartite Pact, 8

Truman, President Harry, 104

Unions. See labor unions

University of Hawai'i, 4

Wainwright, General Jonathan M., head of G2, 34, 46

Wang, Colonel Chih, 47

Willoughby, General Charles A.: commendation of Komori, xv; granted permission to marry, 71; released Honolulu Star Bulletin interview for publication, 69; recommendation of Komori for Purple Heart, 54; recommendation of Komori for Silver Star, 55; statement of Nisei contributions, 108

Wood, Major Stuart, 34, 41

Yamagata, Clarence, 34, 47

Yukimura, Jiro, 98–99